Women and the Cuban Revolution

Women
and the
Cuban
Revolution

Speeches & documents
by Fidel Castro, Vilma Espín & others

Edited by Elizabeth Stone

Pathfinder Press

New York   London   Sydney

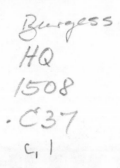

Burgess
HQ
1508
.C37
c, 1

Library of Congress Catalog Card Number 81-85647
ISBN 0-87348-607-2 cloth, 0-87348-608-0 paper
Manufactured in the United States of America
First edition 1981
Third printing 1987

Pathfinder Press
410 West Street, New York, NY 10014
Distributors:
Africa, Europe, and the Middle East:
  Pathfinder Press, 47 The Cut, London SE1 8LL England
Asia, Australia, and the Pacific:
  Pathfinder Press, P.O. Box 37, Leichhardt,
  Sydney, NSW 2040 Australia
Canada:
  DEC Book Distribution, 229 College St., Toronto,
  Ontario M5T 1R4 Canada
New Zealand:
  Pilot Books, Box 8730, Auckland, New Zealand

Contents

Vilma Espín

Fidel Castro

INTRODUCTION

On January 1, 1959, the U.S.-backed dictatorship of Fulgencio Batista was overthrown in Cuba. Working people and peasants, under the leadership of the July 26 Movement, began to shape the economic, social, and political course of that small island to meet the needs of the majority, not the tiny handful of wealthy landowners and businessmen who had dominated Cuba in league with the U.S. corporations and the American government.

When that process began, there was nothing in Cuba resembling what we would today call a women's liberation movement. But the revolutionary struggle itself soon brought about a massive awakening of women. In the early 1960s, millions of women were mobilized to defend the revolution and to carry out tasks aimed at raising the standard of living of the masses of people. For most of these women such activities were the first step out of the home into any kind of social or political life. Their participation opened up a new world to them. The way they looked at themselves began to change. And deeply rooted anti-women prejudices and customs began to be called into question.

Now, over twenty years later, the lives of Cuban women have been transformed. When compared to other underdeveloped countries, the advances toward equality for women in Cuba have been truly dramatic. And on crucial questions like the right to paid maternity leaves, the availability of quality child care, the right to a job, the right to abortion and free medical care for all, and the right to full legal equality, Cuban women are ahead of their sisters in the industrialized capitalist countries.

And the changes are still unfolding. The Cuban people see their revolution as a living process that is still going forward. This is all the more true in an endeavor as far-reaching as ending the oppression of women. Here, it is widely recognized that there is still a long way to go.

The speeches and documents in this book are part of the record of the changes that have taken place thus far. Here, leaders of the revolution analyze the nature of women's oppression and describe the progress made in fighting against it. They also discuss the problems they have faced, the mistakes made, and at each point they project the next steps forward.

Colonial Heritage

To understand the Cuban revolution and the struggle of Cuban women for equality over the last two decades, it is necessary to start with Cuba's heritage as a colonized country. The years of colonial and semicolonial domination—first by Spain, then by the United States—stunted and warped every aspect of Cuba's development. As a result, prior to 1959 Cuban women suffered the extreme oppression that is characteristic of countries dominated by imperialism.

In 1959 only a small percentage of Cuban women held jobs, about 9.8 percent.[1] Economic underdevelopment was reflected not only in this fact but in the kinds of jobs women performed. Some women were secretaries, nurses, or teachers. Others worked in the textile or tobacco industries. But the overwhelming majority of working women—70 percent—were domestic servants.[2]

Those women who worked as maids were often literally slaves to their employers, working long hours, living in the same house so they could be at their beck and call. Many were young women from rural areas, driven by the poverty of the countryside to come to the city to find work.

Many other similarly desperate young women became prostitutes who catered not only to Cubans but to the large numbers of North American tourists, businessmen, and U.S. military personnel stationed at U.S. bases in Cuba.

For the masses of people, men and women alike, life in prerevolutionary Cuba was hard. Malnutrition and hunger were widespread. Half the population lived in thatched huts, shacks, or single-room slum housing. Half the people were without electricity. Half didn't have running water or inside toilets.[3] One quarter were completely illiterate. Chronic unemployment was as high as it was in the U.S. during the depth of the 1930s depression.[4]

Contraception was generally unavailable and abortion was illegal. Even when women were able to obtain birth control devices, husbands often considered the use of them a threat to their manhood. The general lack of medical care meant that 80 percent of all babies were not born in hospitals.[5] Many died at an early age.

Women suffered most from all the effects of underdevelopment. It was they who did household chores without benefit of electricity and running water. They were the ones with the highest rate of illiteracy. The economic stagnation and low level of industrialization—products of imperialist exploitation—meant that it was almost impossible for a woman without education or a skill to get a job except as someone else's personal servant.

Since few women were needed to work in mines, mills, or factories, there was little challenge to the centuries-old myth that women were not suited to work outside the family domain. Women were discouraged from taking part in public life and in many families women were not even allowed to venture out of the house without a chaperone. All the social attitudes generally summed up in the term "machismo" were in full force. A common phrase was, "Women belong in the home, men belong in the street."

This legacy of social and economic backwardness was the greatest obstacle to women's equality. Real changes could only come about based on economic development and the integration of women into social production. Only with this could the deeply held prejudices about women's role be changed. This meant that changes in the situation of women in Cuba had to be made in stages, step by step, as the struggle against underdevelopment progressed.

The Struggle Begins

The women who joined the struggle against the dictator Batista in the 1950s had already begun to show the way. They played an important role in that fight. Women organized demonstrations and worked in the underground, collecting supplies for the guerrillas, selling bonds to raise money, creating hospitals, sewing uniforms, and hiding revolutionaries in their houses. They served as messengers and spies. There are many stories about the role women played in transporting weapons under their skirts through the streets of Santiago and the other centers of revolutionary activity.

Some women became guerrilla fighters. Individual women fought on different guerrilla fronts and there was also a group of women combatants called the Mariana Grajales Platoon, named after the Black woman active in Cuba's first war of independence. This legendary unit grew to the size of a company during the final stages of the revolutionary war and was maintained afterwards.

The women who joined the struggle to overthrow Batista not

only had to have the courage to face the repression and torture of Batista's police, but they also had to buck the prevailing prejudice against women's involvement in politics. Describing the tremendous pressure put on women by their families and others not to participate, Haydée Santamaría, one of the leaders and heroes of the revolution, commented, "My own mother was the kind of woman who thought that men were the only ones who had the right to make revolutions."[6]

Women had to counter the prejudices of their own comrades-in-arms as well. A speech by Fidel Castro, given in Granma Province on January 20, 1981, described the opposition among the male guerrilla fighters to women having a combat role:

"I remember that when I organized the Mariana Grajales Platoon—in fact, I took part in the combat training of those comrades—some of the rebel fighters were furious, because they didn't like the idea of a platoon made up of women. We had some spare M-1s, and the M-1 was considered a good light weapon and, therefore, we thought it would be the right one for the women. Some of our fighters wanted to know why they had Springfields while the women were going to get M-1s. On more than one occasion I got so annoyed that I would answer, 'Because they are better fighters than you are.' And the truth is that they showed it. A large group of women formed part of the troops that marched on Holguín. Near Holguín, a women's platoon engaged in a fierce battle with the army and the platoon leader was wounded. As a general rule, when a platoon leader was wounded the men had the habit of retreating—which is not correct but it had become practically a habit. The women's platoon had attacked a truck loaded with soldiers. When the platoon leader was wounded, they weren't discouraged. They went on fighting, wiped out the truckload and captured all the weapons. Their behavior was truly exceptional."[7]

The women who fought against Batista were pioneers in making changes that were to effect millions of Cuban women later on. In his first speeches immediately after the revolution came to power, Castro paid homage to these women fighters and used their example to explain how the revolution was going to move forward to involve masses of women.

One of the first activities to draw in large numbers of women was the creation of the militia. As the revolution deepened with the carrying out of the land reform and the nationalization of large imperialist holdings, the U.S. government and counterrevolutionaries within Cuba began to organize armed opposition.

Bombings, sabotage of factories, and the burning of sugarcane fields went hand-in-hand with the threat of military attack from the United States. To help counter this a popular militia was organized in the workplaces and schools, and women who worked or who were students joined it.

There was a big hue and cry from counterrevolutionary elements about women's incorporation into the militia. They questioned the "morals" of women who dressed like men, wore pants, and carried guns. When the militia women went out to drill, they were sometimes greeted with rocks. There were also many supporters of the revolution who questioned whether women belonged in the militia. But every able-bodied person was needed to defend the country, and eventually most revolutionaries were won over.

The intensification of the counterrevolutionary attacks led in September 1960 to the formation of the Committees for the Defense of the Revolution (CDRs). Even larger numbers of women joined the CDRs, which were organized on a block-by-block basis. They guarded public buildings, watched for suspicious activities in the neighborhoods, and carried out other important tasks of the revolution.

On August 23, 1960, another big step was taken with the formation of the Federation of Cuban Women (FMC). The FMC immediately began to organize masses of women, house by house, in the cities and the countryside, helping to build the militias and the CDRs, organizing the drive against illiteracy, setting up schools for peasant women, and establishing a network of child-care centers.

Because the FMC was an organization led by and made up entirely of women, those women who had never before participated in politics or other public activity often felt more at home in its ranks. The FMC also provided a place where women could discuss the problems they faced as women and press for changes to alleviate these problems. The accomplishments of the FMC, its dynamism, and the discipline of its members played an important role in raising consciousness about the revolutionary contributions women were making.

In 1961, the campaign to wipe out illiteracy was organized. It was a gigantic effort. A hundred thousand youth between the ages of ten and eighteen left their schools and went into the countryside as literacy *brigadistas* to teach people how to read and write.[8] Over half of these *brigadistas* were girls and young women.

Fifty-five percent of those who learned to read and write were women.[9] This was accomplished despite considerable resistance to including women in the campaign. *Lucia,* a Cuban movie produced in the 1960s, portrays a typical example of such resistance when Lucia's husband tries to prevent her from attending literacy classes and she fights back against this. For thousands of women like Lucia, learning to read was a first step toward greater self-confidence, a sense of their own worth and dignity, and more control over their lives.

For the young women and girls who went out to teach, the experience was a wrenching break from the past. Until then, some of them had not even been allowed out of the house alone. Now they were traveling to the most remote parts of the countryside and mountains, where they shared the life of poverty of the peasants, not only teaching but also working with them in the fields.

One of the slogans of the literacy *brigadistas* was "You will learn more than you teach," and this turned out to be the case. They learned about the peasants' life and work and returned to the cities with a better understanding of why the desperately poor areas of the countryside needed to be given preferential treatment by the revolution.

From the ranks of these teachers came new cadres for the revolution—youth who were more conscious of the challenges that lay ahead and ready to commit themselves to the necessary tasks. The campaign also deepened consciousness about the role of women in the revolution. Years later, one former literacy teacher expressed it this way: "The literacy drive was the first time in my life, and I believe the first time in our history as well, that women were given an equal role with men in bringing about a monumental change."[10]

Along with the literacy drive came other bold educational efforts. A school was set up in Havana for 20,000 maids.[11] As their employers left for the United States, these former maids were trained as child-care workers, bank workers, and taxi and bus drivers.

Special schools were set up for former prostitutes too, where they could live, receive an education, and learn skills which would prepare them to be integrated into the labor force.

Another even bigger project was the Ana Betancourt School for Peasant Girls, set up in 1961. This school was named for a fighter in Cuba's first struggle for independence against Spain, who in 1869 called for equal rights for women.

During the 1960s, tens of thousands of peasant women came from the countryside to Havana and were educated at the Ana Betancourt School, which was housed in mansions abandoned by the rich. A major focus at the school was learning to sew, in part because it was felt that teaching a skill that was both useful and traditional to women would maximize the chances that the families of these young women would allow them to come from the rural areas into Havana. Along with the sewing came classes in reading, writing, history, and an introduction to the goals of the revolution.

To follow up on the literacy drive, a massive adult education program was created, which has been expanded over the years. There was also a crash program to build schools at the elementary, junior high, and high school levels. Not only did new buildings have to be constructed, but large numbers of teachers had to be rapidly recruited and trained. Older children taught younger children. Former literacy *brigadistas* became teachers at the Ana Betancourt peasant schools. At the hastily built teacher-training schools, as soon as a person learned a skill, they were expected to teach it to others. The peasant women who learned to sew were given sewing machines and urged to go back home and teach ten others what they had learned.

The whole educational program involved women in a big way and this is still referred to in Cuba today. Women are proud of their role in constructing the educational system and in expanding that system over the years.

Women also began to get involved in other areas. By the middle 1960s, for example, nearly half the medical students were women.[12] When the medium-sized and large businesses were nationalized, four thousand women were picked to head up workplaces where the majority of workers were women. In many instances women who had never known how to read or write before the revolution ended up carrying big responsibilities in agriculture or industry.

Women were motivated to do all these things because they wanted to be part of the changes which they hoped would lead to a better life for the masses of working people and peasants. They didn't do this with a full consciousness of the need for women's equality. But equal rights was involved. Women were establishing their right to participate, their right to an equal education, their right to be in the militia, their right, as the *brigadista* put it, to be given an equal role in bringing about monumental changes.

Fidel Castro and other leaders often spoke in those years about the important role of women in the revolution. This and educational tools such as the movie *Lucia* helped combat backward attitudes. But the key consciousness-raiser was the experiences of the women themselves. It was their participation and accomplishments that gave women a new consciousness of their worth and political importance. And this confidence grew as more and more people began to realize that the full participation of women was essential to the very survival of the revolution.

Included in this book is a speech by Castro, given in Santa Clara on December 6, 1966, which describes this consciousness-raising process that was taking place.

"In reality," Castro said, "all of us were prejudiced in regard to women.

"And if anyone had ever asked me if I considered myself prejudiced in regard to women, I would have said absolutely not, because I believed myself to be quite the opposite. I believed that an enormous potential force and extraordinary human resources for the revolution existed in our women.

"But what has happened? What has occurred, or rather, what is occurring? We are finding that, in reality, this potential force is superior to anything that the most optimistic of us ever dreamed of. We say that perhaps at heart, unconsciously, something of a bias or underestimation existed."

Castro went on to explain the reason for the strong support among women for the revolution, for their dedication, discipline, and hard work:

"This revolution has really been two revolutions for women; it has meant a double liberation: as part of the exploited sector of the country, and second, as women, who were discriminated against not only as workers but also as women."

Castro added that if women were doubly exploited under capitalism, then in a socialist revolution they would be "doubly revolutionary."

Into the Work Force

The accomplishments of the early years encouraged even greater progress as the 1960s wore on. By 1964, there was no longer the extreme level of unemployment that had plagued the country earlier. A commission was set up to try to encourage more women to take full-time jobs. Around that time the FMC also began to focus on raising consciousness about the importance of incorporating women into the work force.

A big motivation for encouraging women to work full time was the fact that their labor was needed to produce the goods necessary to make life better for everyone. But there was also something else involved. The Cuban leadership understood—as Marxists have long explained—that women's oppression stems from their being confined to the home, isolated from broader social life, economically dependent on their husbands. It was understood that to be fully free, Cuban women not only had to be capable of financially supporting themselves, but also had to take full part in the social, cultural, political, and economic life of the country. This meant participating in all the big tasks of the revolution, such as establishing the national health-care and education systems and building up agriculture, industry, and the military defenses of the revolution.

An important first step toward the integration of women into the work force was the voluntary labor carried out by women throughout the 1960s. To help overcome the economic shortages and dislocations caused by the U.S. economic blockade, masses of Cubans volunteered to go to the countryside on weekends or for longer periods of time to pick crops, weed, or do whatever was needed. There were many special FMC brigades to carry out such tasks.

For most women, this voluntary labor was their first work experience and many found they enjoyed being able to work around others, with the comraderie and sense of achievement this involved. These experiences made it easier for them later to counter the objections of their husbands, and their own hesitations as well, about working full time.

Beginning in 1968, a new stage in the incorporation of women into the work force began with the initiation of a gigantic campaign, led by the FMC, to bring 100,000 new women into the full-time work force each year.

During this campaign, FMCers went door to door and talked with over 600,000 women and their families, urging the women either to go to work or to enroll in educational classes.[13] Along with these individual discussions, the campaign included the publication of pamphlets on women's role in carrying through the socialist revolution in Cuba, assemblies where this was discussed, and radio messages and billboards which proclaimed: "Women, the revolution in the revolution" and "The revolution of women is greater than the revolution itself."

A part of this effort was the passage in 1968 of two laws known as Resolutions 47 and 48. Resolution 47 stipulated that women were to be given first choice in certain job categories. Men were asked to leave these jobs so that women could take them. Resolution 48 specified certain jobs that were to be reserved for men, since they were considered physically harmful to women. The aim of both resolutions was to make it easier to draw more women into the work force, and this purpose was achieved. At the same time, the problems that would inevitably result from creating rigid categories of work for men and women soon became obvious. Resolution 47 was ended by a decision of the 1973 congress of the Central Organization of Cuban Trade Unions after it became clear there were not enough women working to fill the jobs set aside for them. Resolution 48, which prohibited women from taking jobs that required lifting heavy weights and other things considered harmful to their health, also had to be changed when it was shown that many women could and wanted to do these jobs. Over time, the number of jobs not done by women because they were considered dangerous to their health has been greatly scaled down.

During these years many advances were made in breaking down old stereotypes about what kinds of jobs women could and could not do. Women became doctors, engineers, and technicians. Women also began to work in the sugar mills and other industries. Some women began to cut cane, a job that is particularly demanding physically. Brigades of women cane cutters were formed, with special recognition being given to the best cutters.

At the same time, many of the old ideas about what work is proper for men and women remain. Although many Cuban women work industrial jobs, there has not been the type of big push by Cuban women, as has developed in the United States, with regard to winning the right to work industrial jobs traditionally done by men. One reason, of course, is the fact that unlike in the U.S., the pay for these jobs is generally not higher than pay in sectors where larger numbers of women are concentrated.

The FMC campaign to incorporate new women into the labor force was greeted with enthusiasm. Thousands of women talked to by the FMC agreed to "step forward" as it was called when a woman agreed to take a job. But, as the months wore on, it became clear that the goal of increasing the total number of women workers by 100,000 a year was not going to be met. At the same time that large numbers of women were entering the work force, large numbers were also dropping out. So many dropped out, in fact, that in the years between 1969 and 1974, although 713,924 women took jobs, the net increase was only 196,903. Thus, in 1974, the percentage of the female population working still only came to 24 percent.

Why did this happen? In her main report to the Second Congress of the FMC, Vilma Espín listed the reasons:

"• Pressure of home and family

"• Lacks in existing services

"• Lack of economic incentive

"• Lack of minimal conditions of hygiene and protection at worksites

"• Lack of political work with the newly incorporated women on the job

"• A lack of understanding concerning women's role in society."[14]

Some of the problems Espín refers to were unavoidable. Cuba was and is still a poor country. In the late 1960s and early 1970s the effects of the U.S. economic blockade were being felt especially keenly. There was not enough cement and other construction material to build the number of child-care centers, laundries, school lunchrooms, workers' dining halls, boarding schools, and take-out restaurants needed to alleviate the burden of housework. In addition to this, Cuban women did not have easy access to consumer goods that make housework easier: refrigerators, washing machines, and so forth. Women were doing their laundry by hand and suffering from other inconveniences such as a poor transportation system and long lines at stores, which stemmed from the economic shortages imposed on Cuba by the U.S. blockade.

There was also insufficient economic incentive to encourage women to work. More money was in circulation than there were goods that people could buy. Everything was rationed to assure a fair distribution, so a second household income often did not mean an equivalent ability to purchase things the family needed. Education, medical care, and many other social services were free and rents were no more than 10 percent of income. This also lessened the need for a second income.

In addition, as Espín pointed out, there were problems stemming from backward attitudes in regard to a woman's right to work. Many husbands pressured their wives to stay home and most refused to share the burden of housework. There was also a lack of support on the part of many workplace administrators who resented giving women time off to care for sick children or meet other responsibilities.

All this meant that even many of the most conscious women

found it too difficult to work full time. They preferred to contribute to the revolution through voluntary part-time projects and by being active in organizations such as the CDRs and the FMC.

In 1974, another event put the spotlight on the situation of women in Cuba. The first election for the governing bodies known in Cuba as the assemblies of People's Power took place in Matanzas Province.* In this experimental first run which paved the way for island-wide elections in 1976, only 7.6 percent of the candidates nominated were women and only 3 percent of those elected were women. So in his July 26, 1974, speech in Matanzas given after the election, Fidel Castro drew attention to this and condemned the fact that more women had not been elected, calling for a study to find out what had happened.

The results of the study pointed to the same problems that were keeping women from holding jobs. Women said they did not have time to serve as People's Power delegates because they were too busy with household tasks. Prejudice was also clearly involved. The study showed that despite the problem of double duties, a much higher percentage of women were capable and willing to serve than were elected.

A New Stage

After the People's Power elections and the drive to get more women into the work force, another stage opened up in the struggle for women's equality and for the incorporation of women into public life. At the Second Congress of the FMC in 1974 and at the First Congress of the Communist Party of Cuba the following year, big discussions took place on how next to advance the struggle for women's equality. Out of these discussions, the following measures were projected:

1. To lighten the burden of women by building more cafeterias in the workplaces and at schools, more laundries, and greatly expanding child-care centers, boarding schools, and other educational facilities.

2. To revive a Women's Front in the unions to work with factory committees, child-care centers, and other institutions to try to solve the problems women workers faced in connection with their jobs. A member of the Women's Front was to sit on the

*People's Power is organized on the local, regional, and national levels. At the local level, delegates are chosen in elections that must have at least two candidates who are nominated by community meetings.

executive committee of the trade union in every workplace.

3. To make things easier for working women by taking a number of special steps. For example, women were to be favored when workers voted on who should get home appliances distributed through the union local. The "plan jaba" (shopping-bag plan) was set up, which gave working women priority for service in the stores and allowed women to leave their shopping bags, with lists of items wanted, at the grocery store on the way to work and pick up the filled bags on the way home.

4. A drive to continue to improve the educational level and technical skills of women was projected.

5. An ideological campaign was opened up to educate the whole population on women's rights and on the need for men to help women with the housework.

The ideological campaign was central to this entire effort and had a number of different aspects to it. First came discussions throughout the island on the passage of the Family Code, which was proposed as a replacement for the prerevolutionary laws on marriage, divorce, adoption, and alimony. Much of the discussion on the Family Code centered on Articles 24 through 28, which stipulated that women should be equal in marriage and that men should share in housework and raising children. This section of the code also stated that both members of a couple should have an equal right to pursue an education or have a job and that they should cooperate with each other to make that possible.

Discussion on the code took place at the grass-roots level in the mass organizations—the FMC, CDRs, and the trade unions. There was also a great deal of informal discussion on street corners, in shopping lines, or wherever people got together. Although the government leadership put its authority behind the code, there were many Cubans, men in particular, who strongly objected. For example, a typical comment made by one military officer was that after sacrificing the best years of his life fighting for the revolution, "I'll be damned if I'm going to do housework." Another remark often heard from the recalcitrants was that "there are some things even Fidel cannot change." But the women and their supporters argued back. And the Family Code was passed by the vote of an overwhelming majority of the population with Articles 24 to 28 included. The code became law on March 8, 1975, International Women's Day.

A second aspect of the ideological campaign was the attention given to the Second Congress of the Federation of Cuban Women in November 1974. Throughout the island, people were made aware of the congress through billboards, posters, and an exhibition about women that was shown in Havana. A film was produced for the occasion portraying the contributions of women to the revolution—women fighting in the Sierra Maestra, carrying out international missions, doing voluntary labor, managing farms, working as technicians, participating in the military, and guarding the country's coasts. It also showed both men and women doing housework.

At the congress itself, the questions made so obvious by the Matanzas election and the campaign to get women into the work force were discussed. Concrete solutions were projected, including the need for more child-care facilities, more cafeterias for workers and students, more laundries, and more of other social services. The need to continue the fight against antiwomen prejudices was also discussed. FMCers called for ending sexist images of women in the media and spoke out against the practice of choosing queens for the carnivals, labeling these as "beauty contests with a red varnish." After the congress, such contests were eliminated in Cuba.

The spirit at the congress was one of exuberation at the progress being made in defining the new problems women were facing and doing something about them. The congress continually exploded in cheers and standing ovations.

A year after the FMC congress, another important discussion on women took place at the First Congress of the Communist Party of Cuba. The discussion centered on a document entitled *Thesis: On the Full Exercise of Women's Equality.* This document, which is reprinted in this book, is the most important and comprehensive statement on women's equality produced by the revolution. It points to the reasons for women's oppression historically, presents facts and figures on the gains made by the revolution, and projects the next steps to be taken. The *Thesis,* which was studied at workplaces, in schools, in the military, and in the CDR and FMC meetings, provided another occasion for a discussion within the population as a whole about the struggle for women's rights.

More Progress

In the years following the discussion at the FMC and CP congresses, steps were taken to act on the proposals made. Child-care facilities amost doubled, increasing the number of children enrolled from 54,382 in 1975[15] to 96,000 in 1981.[16] More than 970 new schools were built, 258 of them being junior and senior high schools in the countryside.[17] More schools and workplaces began to supply meals. And the percentage of women working rose from 25 to 32 percent of the work force.

A number of economic problems have been overcome since 1975. More families have access to home appliances. The number of refrigerators per 100 homes with electricity has risen from 15 in 1975 to 38 in 1980, while the number of washing machines went from 6 to 34 per 100 homes.

Rationing of food and consumer items continues, but a wide and growing range of goods is also available off ration, including sports equipment, radios, televisions, clothes, and some kinds of shoes. With more goods available, there is more direct economic incentive for women to work.

Women in Cuba are also benefiting from a very advanced maternity-rights law that was passed in 1974. The law provides for eighteen weeks of paid leave—six weeks before birth and twelve weeks after—with eighteen other days off before and after birth for prenatal medical check-ups and for taking the newborn baby to the doctor. And if a woman wants, she can take a year's leave without pay and still be able to return to her former job.

Due to the excellent public health-care system, there has also been a big improvement in care at the maternity hospitals. The infant mortality rate has been reduced to 19.4 per 1,000 live births, the lowest in Latin America and comparable to the levels in the most economically advanced countries. (It is worth noting that this is lower than in many parts of the United States; in Washington, D.C., for example, the infant mortality rate is 24.6.) Special live-in maternity hospitals have been built in rural areas too isolated for a woman to get to a hospital after labor begins. Women spend the last weeks of their pregnancies at these hospitals and use that time to learn how to care for their newborn babies.

Women have the right to abortion on demand, free of charge as are all medical services. Public clinics also make contraception free and available to all women, regardless of marital status. There are no campaigns in Cuba to pressure women either to cut down or to expand the number of children they have. This is considered a matter of personal choice.

There has been some progress on the election of women to leadership positions although this is still viewed as an area of weakness. In the second national People's Power elections in April 1979 the percentage of women elected was actually lower than the 6.6 percent elected in the October 1976 elections. However, in the October 1981 elections, the percentage of women elected rose slightly to 7.9 percent.

The number of women elected to be members of the Communist Party, which is a big honor and responsibility in Cuba, rose from 14.1 percent in 1975 to 19.1 percent in 1980.[19] The number of women in top leadership positions in the party is still quite low and the deaths of veteran leaders Celia Sánchez and Haydée Santamaría in 1980 left holes that will be difficult to fill. At the same time, a special step was taken at the CP's Second Congress held in 1980 to incorporate more women into the higher bodies of the party.

It is significant that among working women the percentage of women aspiring to leadership is greater than in the population as a whole. Women account for 42.7 percent of the leadership of the trade unions at the local level.[20] Among the youth, the consciousness on this question is also more advanced. Almost 42 percent of the members of the Young Communist League are women, up from 30 percent in 1975.[21]

Women in Cuba are not subject to the draft, but many serve in the armed forces and some young women attend military training schools. Most recently, there has been a drive to incorporate large numbers of women into the territorial militias, which were set up in 1981 in response to the escalating U.S. threats against Cuba.

Rape and violent crimes against women are nowhere near as prevalent in Cuba as they are in the United States. Cuban women are truly horrified to hear that women in the U.S. feel unsafe walking the streets at night. This is something that is not in their experience.

Since the revolution crime of all types has decreased. Members of the CDRs still do regular guard duty in the neighborhoods to guard against counterrevolutionary sabotage such as bombings (which still take place) as well as petty theft or problems such as violent arguments that could lead to physical confrontation. These CDR guards play an important role in making things safer for everyone.

Cuba is also largely free of the omnipresent pornography that mixes sex with violence, which can been seen in U.S. films, TV, and advertising. Since Cuba is free of advertising in general, you don't see women's bodies being used to sell products.

Since 1975, the ideological campaign to raise consciousness about women's rights has continued. *Portrait of Teresa,* a film produced in 1979, sparked a big discussion in Cuba about women's rights and about the question of using a double standard for men and women with regard to sex. The film also portrayed the main problem that many working women in Cuba still contend with—husbands who do not do housework and the *triple* burden they have of a job, housework, and political activities and other interests outside the home.

As one would expect, among the youth housework is shared more equally. But the older generation is slower to change. One veteran of the struggle against Batista who is now a government official put it this way: "My wife works. But when I help her with the housework I feel like a saint. I should not feel this way. The tasks of the home should be our mutual problem. And I am still one of the best on this."

The main source of the many problems that still exist is Cuba's economic limitations—the legacy of imperialist domination and the twenty-year trade embargo. The material resources to provide the number of child-care centers and other services needed to free women from their domestic chores are simply not available.

Thirty-two percent of women working is a high figure for an underdeveloped country. The systematic way in which women have been encouraged and helped to enter the work force shows the superiority of a planned economy such as Cuba's. At the same time, when measured against the goal of winning complete equality for women, the percentage is relatively low. When the number of women going to school full time and of old people who are not working is subtracted, this still leaves a very large number of women in Cuba who do housework and rear children as their main job. This reality holds back consciousness in regard to women's rights. It helps perpetuate the stereotype that child raising and household tasks are "women's work." And it makes it harder to tackle questions of prejudice and discrimination at every level—whether it be a double standard in sexual relations or the question of electing more women to leadership positions.

It is necessary to keep this in mind when comparing the dynamic of the struggle for women's rights in Cuba with the way the women's liberation movement has unfolded in the U.S. and other industrialized capitalist countries. The accelerated expansion of world capitalism in the 1950s and '60s opened up large numbers of jobs for women in these countries. In addition, the employers' offensive against the real standard of living of working people during the 1970s pressured even more women into taking jobs, to the extent that the majority of working-age women are now in the labor market, with women making up 42 percent of the total U.S. work force.

The women's liberation movement in the U.S. arose in the late 1960s out of the growing contradiction between the reality of women's lives—the fact that they are more likely to be working outside the home and receiving more education, while at the same time they are being discriminated against in every area.

Prior to 1959 there had been no similar expansion of Cuba's economy. Cuban women thus did not face the same kinds of contradictions. These began to develop only when large numbers of women were able to get an education and enter the labor force. Only then were such questions as whether men should do housework posed as social issues. Only then did masses of women begin to gain the confidence and consciousness necessary to think in terms of a goal of *complete* equality for women in every area of society.

The Revolutionary Framework of the Struggle

The struggle of women for equal rights in Cuba is a process. At every stage, underdevelopment has placed obstacles along the way. But since 1959 there have been big leaps forward in all areas—from the right to an education, a job, paid maternity leaves, child care, and abortion to getting rid of prostitution and ending degrading practices such as beauty contests and sexist advertising.

Such impressive gains could not have been achieved except within the context of a deepgoing revolution which not only challenged the oppression of women, but set out to eradicate capitalism—an economic system whose motive force is maximizing profit for a tiny handful who own the productive resources of society—and replace it with an economic system based on maximizing the well-being of all. Every single gain Cuban women have made—whether it has been the right to a job or free abortion and contraception or equal education—has come about as part of this broader revolutionary transformation aimed at improving the lives and standard of living of the masses of Cuban workers and peasants.

The women who were most oppressed before the revolution— Black women, poor peasants, agricultural workers, prostitutes, maids, and the urban poor—have benefited most from this process.

Before the revolution, discrimination against Black women was severe. Segregation existed in public areas and facilities such as hotels and beaches, and Black women had an even harder time than their sisters in getting a job. Black women were excluded from some of the more sought-after occupations such as nursing.

Now racial discrimination and segregation in jobs, schooling, housing, and recreational facilities is a thing of the past in Cuba. Some racist attitudes still exist, especially among older people, and the effects of the legacy of centuries of Black oppression have not been fully eradicated. But the whole revolutionary climate of Cuba—the internationalism, the solidarity with liberation struggles in Africa, and the opposition to racism and chauvinism of any kind—helps to counteract this and puts Cuba in the vanguard of the fight against racism internationally.

In Cuba today there is no capitalist ruling class which seeks to profit from racism or sexism and there is no capitalist drive to roll back gains already won in order to improve profit margins.

Masses of Cubans have taken part in discussions about women's rights in their CDRs, the FMC, and the assemblies of People's Power, and voted on what course should be taken to bring this about. And masses of working people and peasants have participated directly in bringing about the needed changes through activities such as the campaign to bring women into the work force.

There is nothing that dramatizes the interrelationship between the class struggle and the struggle of women in Cuba better than the commitment of the Cuban government to the expansion of social services such as child care. While the government in the U.S. is cutting back on such things as education, health-care benefits, pensions for old people, and aid to the handicapped, Cuba continues to devote more and more resources to such services. And there is a strong emphasis on trying to make public institutions and services of as high a quality as possible.

The nature of the child-care centers is a prime example of this. Children at the centers are provided with clothes, bathed, given nutritious meals, and provided with regular medical examinations, shots, and dental care. Psychiatric care is also provided where needed.

The purpose of such centers is not simply that of baby-sitting while parents work, but to promote the full intellectual, physical, and social growth of the children. There is also a conscious attempt to develop in them a social consciousness. For example, children learn about how workers and farmers produce the food and other products they use, and they are taught to value the contributions made by all those who work. Children learn to share with each other, are taught to respect each other, and to identify with children of other countries.

The long-term goal is for all preschool children to be able to go to such centers, where they can benefit from an environment structured especially for them—with facilities, toys, and an experience with other children that an individual home cannot provide. Even infants benefit from the collective experience at the centers and babies are accepted from the age of 45 days on.

At the grade school level, there is also a concern for the rounded development of children. This is reflected in the activities of the Pioneers, the children's organization that carries out activities in the schools, after school, and during summer vacations. Pioneer camps have been built throughout the country, some in beautiful locations on the beach or in the mountains. The Pioneers go to the camps for after-school activities and during summer vacation. All kinds of skills are taught at the camps—everything from karate to dairy farming and how to run a radio station. And all this is, of course, completely free.

Another inspiring innovation for youth of the junior high school level are the hundreds of boarding schools in the country-side. The youth at these schools are put in charge of agricultural projects and spend part of the day working in the fields and the other part studying, going to classes, and taking part in sports and other recreational activities. The guiding principle for this type of school, as it is for all Cuban education, is that of combining physical work with study. At every grade level, young people in Cuba participate in some kind of manual labor. Even the preschool and grade school youngsters help tend little gardens.

The aim of work-study is to teach children from an early age to value physical work and to respect the contributions of all those who do work. Work-study also gives young people a chance to learn by doing, as well as through reading. By participating in large-scale agricultural production, these students learn to solve problems and meet challenges usually reserved only for adults.

Work-study also helps break down sex roles, since both boys and girls pitch in to do the work. At boarding school all the students work together to clean, wash clothes, iron, and take care of other tasks traditionally relegated to women.

In Cuba there is a firm commitment to coeducation, which extends from the level of child care through adult education classes. This is even true of the sports schools where high school-level youth are trained to become teachers of physical education. Almost all the gym classes are conducted with men and women together. Exceptions to the general rule of coeducation are the nurses-training schools and the schools for child-care teachers, where old role stereotypes still hang on, creating student bodies entirely female in composition.

Cuba's massive free educational system, with its child care, adult educational programs, boarding schools, Pioneer camps, sports programs, and free meals, not only makes a big contribution to freeing women from housework, but is at the same time a big gain for the working class as a whole. Such a use of the country's resources brings with it not only more equality for women but a better life for all workers. It is the opposite of the situation under capitalism, where each individual family is responsible to pay for such things as medical care or child care, with rich families and their children getting the best and working-class families making do as best they can.

The Cuban Family

The changes brought about by the elimination of capitalist property relations have had a big impact on the family unit, helping to put relations between family members on a healthier basis. Before the revolution, a divorce was not easy to get and marriage was a matter of economic survival for women. Millions of women in those days remained married to husbands they did not particularly like, or maybe even hated and feared, because they had no economic alternative.

Now, with jobs and child care available, there is a new degree of choice. Many women of the older generations in Cuba will tell you that for them the right to freely choose a marriage partner and leave one with whom they did not want to live was one of the most important gains of the revolution. Some revolutionaries express this more poetically. They say that "the revolution saved love."

It is easy to get a divorce in Cuba today. The divorce rate increased from 8.5 per 100 marriages in 1959 to 30.2 per 100 in 1974.[22] The number of marriages also dramatically increased after the revolution. Up until 1959 marriage was a luxury reserved for those with money.

With contraception available and free, there is also a greater sexual freedom than before. Many couples live together without getting married and this is becoming increasingly accepted. There is still a double standard in relation to sex, but less so among the youth. The *Thesis* passed at the first Communist Party congress calls for using the same sexual standard for men and women.

Relations within the family are evolving too. The old norm, where a tyrannical father dominated wife and children, is becoming a thing of the past. Articles 24 to 28 of the Family Code, calling for equal rights for marriage partners and for sharing household tasks, have been incorporated into the marriage vows.

Child care, summer camp, and the various Pioneer activities have helped give children more self-confidence and independence. The boarding schools for junior and senior high school students also play a big role in this. Parents and youth both say they like the extra room which a boarding school provides for young people to establish their own identities at a crucial period in their lives. Learning to cope away from home, working and studying, not only builds the students' self-respect but also builds mutual respect and the basis for a warmer relationship between youth and their parents.

Many parents whose children are in boarding school today participated in the literacy drive in the early 1960s. Their sons and daughters now feel that by going to the countryside and joining the battle against underdevelopment they are carrying on a revolutionary tradition and making the same kind of contribution their parents made as youth.

As of now, 283,000 junior high school–age youth attend boarding school[23] and the goal is to raise this figure from the current 35.7 percent to over 40 percent by 1985.[24] Attendance at the schools is voluntary and there never have been enough places to satisfy the demand. Some parents, of course, still have mixed feelings about having their children leave home, but the fact that the students come home to visit on weekends helps to win acceptance for this.

Along with the changes taking place within the family, there has at the same time been a big stress on the importance of the family as the basic cell of society. One of the aims of the Family Code is "the strengthening of the family and of the ties of affection and reciprocal respect between its members."

Cubans are urged to take their commitments related to marriage and the family very seriously, especially when children are involved. Bringing up children continues to be a big responsibility and men and women alike are urged to take the time to give their children the necessary care and attention.

The extended family continues to be very strong. Different generations often live in the same household, in many cases due to the housing shortage. Grandparents, relatives, and friends play a big role in baby-sitting for children whose parents both work when child care is not available.

While there has been steady progress in integrating women into the work force, great pains have been taken to make it clear that it is *up to the woman to decide* whether she wants to, or is able to, work at a paid job. This is especially important given the limited child care and the fact that housework continues to be a heavy burden.

This question came up in 1970 when an antiloafing law was passed which stipulated that all able-bodied men who enjoy the economic fruits of society should be required to work. Women were exempted from the law to make it clear that they already contribute to the welfare of society, and that it is their choice whether to work outside the home as well.

The Cuban leadership's stance of working to strengthen ties of affection and respect between family members has caused some writers on Cuba to question whether they are rejecting the traditional Marxist position that the family is first and foremost an *economic* institution, and as such is responsible for the oppression of women. But in all essentials the Cubans have acted in accord with the analysis of Marx, Engels, and Lenin on this question. In his famous work, *The Origin of the Family, Private Property, and the State,* Engels puts forward the same goals the Cubans have stressed as being necessary to freeing women: 1) ending the economic dependence of women on their husbands; 2) getting women out of the isolation of the home and incorporating them into the work force; 3) socializing household chores traditionally done by women through the use of public laundries, cafeterias, child care, and other public services; and 4) ending the *economic* chains that compel family members to remain together, so that relationships between people can be based on affection and not on economic necessity.

The Cubans have not only taken very radical positions on these questions, but they have made important headway in moving in this direction, despite their economic problems. In fact, one of the most revolutionary aspects of the transformation of Cuban society has been precisely the many varied and imaginative ways in which the Cubans have socialized tasks and responsibilities traditionally borne by the family. A list of just some of the types of things the Cubans have put into effect in this regard would include the following: free medical care; rents which are a maximum of 10 percent of a family's income; inexpensive restaurants and cafeterias where take-out food is available; free or inexpensive lunches in workplaces and schools; programs to socialize care for the elderly such as homes for the aged, special vacation resorts, centers for old people, and providing decent pensions; boarding schools at all levels including for some primary students; Pioneer programs, camps, and other after-school activities; inexpensive vacation resorts where workers and peasants can take their families; free amateur sports programs and free sports events; museums and cultural activities of all kinds that are free of charge; programs for amateur poets, writers, musicians, and artists; free adult education; child care; free dental care; free psychiatric care for anyone who needs it; free schools for handicapped children; free summer camps for children with asthma; and so forth.

Programs such as these not only make life easier and better for the masses of people, but they also help lessen the economic dependence of family members on each other. This goal is stated clearly in the *Programmatic Platform of the Communist Party of Cuba,* which states: "It is fundamental for the family to adopt as its own the principles of morality and education upheld by our revolution, gradually eliminating the elements of material dependence among its members, and consolidating itself on the basis of common spiritual interests."[25]

This approach of the Cubans is the complete opposite of the reactionary "profamily" forces in the U.S., who sing praises to the family at the same time they cut back social services, thus making it harder for members of working-class families to survive. The increased burdens that women shoulder in this situation and the tensions that flow from the growing financial pressures only serve to heighten animosities between family members and lead to increases in alchoholism, drug addiction, suicides, and homicides, as well as wife-beating and child abuse.

A Transitional Period

Cuba is in a period of transition. Capitalist property relations have been eliminated. New economic and social relations are being forged. There has been steady progress. At the same time, there is a consciousness that there is still a long way to go.

The Cuban people recognize that the ultimate success of their fight for complete freedom for women, as well as equality and abundance for all the people of Cuba, is dependent not just on the hard work they do to develop their own country, but on the success of the world revolution as well. As a small island, it is impossible for them to solve their economic problems without the increased trade and aid that will come as a result of socialist revolutions elsewhere.

Cubans have been especially inspired by the revolutions in Nicaragua and Grenada and the role played by women in these struggles. It was a great day in Cuba when fresh from the revolutionary victory in Nicaragua, a large delegation of Sandinistas, including a number of prominent women fighters, came to Cuba to celebrate Cuba's revolutionary holiday on July 26, 1979.

In many ways Nicaraguan women have gone beyond what Cuban women were able to accomplish at the beginning of their revolution. It is estimated that 30 percent of the guerrilla fighters in the war against the dictator Somoza were women, and today women continue to play a big role in rebuilding the country and defending it from the U.S.-inspired and financed counterrevolution. In contrast to Cuba in its early years, the big majority of Nicaraguan women are in the labor force. In the capital city of Managua, 54 percent of the total work force are women.[26]

At the same time, because of the extreme devastation brought about by the civil war and the 1972 earthquake that destroyed much of the capital city, Nicaraguan women face as big a challenge, if not bigger, than their Cuban sisters in building up the economic basis for freeing women. Not only do they inherit an extremely poor country, but they will also face all the problems Cuba faced arising from Washington's attempts to overthrow the revolution.

Cuban women were the first in Latin America to successfully break the chains of imperialism and begin to forge their own history. They were real pioneers not only because they were the first, but also because in 1959 there was no international women's movement as exists in the world today.

The Cuban women of this older pioneering generation are now among the staunchest supporters of the revolution. They are veterans of the struggles and they also know best how the lives of women have been changed by the revolution. Now they are being joined by younger women who have been raised with the revolution and who have even more confidence in themselves and more far-reaching goals. These young women believe they are also making history through working to overcome underdevelopment, by joining the militia, by going abroad to teach or give other types of aid to countries such as Nicaragua and Angola. Of the first detachment of 1,200 teachers who went to Nicaragua to participate in the literacy drive there, half were women.

The spirit of this new generation was captured in a comment made to the U.S. educator Jonathan Kozol by a young junior high school boarding student. She told him: "For a long time women were not in positions to assert themselves. Nowadays in our country we can take an equal stand. So reading in the past means mainly reading about men. But I can tell you one thing: It won't be that way for long!"[27]

Elizabeth Stone
November 1981

Notes

1. Margaret Randall, *Cuban Women Now* (Toronto: The Women's Press, 1974), p. 9.

2. Margaret Randall, *Women in Cuba* (Brooklyn: Smyrna Press, 1981), p. 23.

3. *Cuba Today: 20 Years of Building Socialism* (Havana: Editorial de Ciencias Sociales, 1979), p. 38.

4. Fidel Castro, *First Congress of the Communist Party of Cuba* (Moscow: Progress Publishers, 1976), pp. 128, 158.

5. *Children in Cuba: Twenty Years of Revolution* (Havana: Editorial de Ciencias Sociales, 1979), p. 37.

6. Randall, *Cuban Women Now*, p. 317.

7. *Granma Weekly Review,* February 1, 1981, p. 3.

8. Jonathan Kozol, *Children of the Revolution* (New York: Dell Publishing Co., 1980), p. 9.

9. Vilma Espín, "Central Report" in *Memories, Second Congress, Cuban Women's Federation* (Havana: Editorial Orbe, 1975), p. 101.

10. Kozol, p. 38.

11. Randall, *Cuban Women Now,* p. 13.

12. Fidel Castro, *Major Speeches* (London: Stage I, 1968), p. 38.

13. Federation of Cuban Women, "Thesis" in *Memories, Second Congress, Cuban Women's Federation,* p. 33.

14. Espín, "Central Report," *Memories,* p. 116.

15. Castro, *First Congress,* p. 151.

16. *Granma Weekly Review,* July 5, 1981, p. 2.

17. Fidel Castro, *Main Report, Second Congress of the Communist Party of Cuba* (New York: Center for Cuban Studies), p. 8.

18. *Ibid.,* p. 7.

19. *Ibid.,* p. 27.

20. *Ibid.,* p. 23.

21. *Ibid.,* p. 26.

22. Nicola Murray, "Socialism and Feminism: Women and the Cuban Revolution" in *Feminist Review,* No. 2, 1979, p. 64.

23. *Granma Weekly Review,* July 5, 1981, p. 2.

24. Castro, *Main Report,* p. 15.

25. *Programmatic Platform of the Communist Party of Cuba* (Havana: Department of Revolutionary Orientation of the Central Committee of the Communist Party of Cuba, 1976), p. 98.

26. *Intercontinental Press/Inprecor,* October 12, 1981, p. 1002.

27. Kozol, p. 27.

Peasant family before the revolution

The Early Years

Vilma Espín

Cubans have a long history of struggle against foreign domination. Following the "discovery" of the island by Christopher Columbus in 1492, Cuba was turned into a Spanish colony, with the native population being wiped out in the process. Thousands of Africans were then brought to Cuba to work as slaves.

Cuba's first war against Spanish domination, known as the Ten Years War, was initiated in 1868. Although this rebellion of the mambí forces—as the Cuban fighters were known—was unsuccessful, it solidified Cubans' desire for independence.

Under the inspiration of the revolutionary essayist and poet José Martí—now one of Cuba's national heroes—a new war for independence broke out in 1895. The Cubans were on the verge of defeating the Spanish when the United States, newly emerging as an imperialist power, entered the war, finished off Spain, and installed an occupation army on Cuban soil.

Although Cuba was granted its formal independence in 1902, the U.S. government imposed the Platt Amendment on Cuba's constitution, giving Washington the right to intervene—including militarily—in Cuban affairs whenever it wanted to. This initiated a bitter period that Cubans refer to as the "pseudorepublic." One repressive government was installed after another under Washington's tutelage. Popular discontent became so great that in 1933 a revolt erupted that drove the tyrant who was then in power, Gerardo Machado, out of office. However, after the upsurge had concluded the neocolonial regime itself remained.

In 1952, Fulgencio Batista, who had been in and out of power during the 1930s and '40s, seized control once again through a military coup, setting up a brutal dictatorship completely subservient to the U.S. government and corporations. In response, a group of young Cuban patriots, led by a 26-year-old lawyer named Fidel Castro, attacked the Moncada army barracks in Santiago de Cuba on July 26, 1953, hoping to provoke a popular uprising. Although unsuccessful, this action marked the beginning of the struggle against Batista and together with Castro's *stirring defense speech, "History Will Absolve Me" and his courageous conduct during his trial and imprisonment, inspired a whole generation of Cuban youth.*

After being released and going into exile in Mexico, Castro organized a group of revolutionary fighters who would become the nucleus of the Rebel Army. They sailed to Cuba on the yacht Granma, landing in eastern Cuba in December 1956. From the nearby Sierra Maestra mountains, they conducted a successful revolutionary war that led to the collapse of Batista's regime on January 1, 1959.

The new government began to institute measures to benefit Cuba's workers and peasants: an agrarian reform that eliminated the large landed properties, an urban reform that nationalized urban real estate and lowered rents, laws banning racial discrimination, a campaign to build hospitals and schools, and the nationalization of foreign financial interests.

The revolution's actions in defense of the rights of the Cuban people provoked the unbridled hostility of the U.S. government. Counterrevolutionary guerrilla forces were organized, a massive campaign of propaganda and disinformation was unleashed, assassination attempts against Castro and other revolutionary leaders were organized, as were efforts to destroy and sabotage Cuba's economy. An economic blockade was imposed by Washington in an attempt to starve Cuba into submission. And in April 1961, the U.S. government, using Cuban exiles, launched an invasion of Cuba at the Bay of Pigs, which was crushed within 72 hours.

*   *   *

Vilma Espín was an active fighter against the Batista tyranny. She was an important figure in the underground movement in Santiago de Cuba, coordinating clandestine work for the July 26 Movement in Oriente Province. She later went up to the Sierra Maestra, where she had a number of responsibilities with the Rebel Army. She has been president of the Federation of Cuban Women since its founding in 1960 and is a member of the Central Committee of the Communist Party of Cuba.

*   *   *

This section includes excerpts from two accounts by Vilma Espín of the history of women's participation in the revolution. The first one was printed in Cuba Socialista, *December 1961; the translation is by Michael Taber. The second is an excerpt from Espín's main report to the FMC's Second Congress in November 1974. It is reprinted from* Memories, Second Congress, Cuban Women's Federation, *(Havana: Editorial Orbe, 1975). As has been done throughout the book, minor changes have been made to correct translation errors and for stylistic consistency.*

"The experience of all liberation movements has shown that the success of a revolution depends on how much the women take part in it." —Lenin

There is a tradition in Cuba of women being present, together with their people, in the struggle for liberation.

A century ago, under the humiliating colonial oppression, women joined in the battles for emancipation. "It can be said that the wars for the island's independence were wars of the entire family. Women took to the hills with the *guajiros*,* taking their families with them," Mirta Aguirre pointed out. In the jungles they shared the dangers with their husbands with admirable tenacity, feeding and caring for the wounded, carrying out a thousand tasks that made the hard fight of the revolutionary soldiers more bearable.

Many anonymous Cuban women took this road, in which the gigantic and heroic figure of Mariana Grajales stands out: humble, Black peasant woman—the true example of the *mambisa* mother.

Already in the Guáimaro Assembly,** the voice of Ana Betancourt reflects Cuban women's preoccupation with their rights being juridically recognized; and in her words, women had to "break their yoke and extend their wings."

The just revolution initiated at Yara,*** which granted freedom to the Black slave, also filled with hope the white woman—accustomed to the comfort of the home. Women's position of inferiority to men was more pronounced among the poor, and even more so among Black women, tied to the oppressive domestic burdens and the care of husband and children. They

* A rustic term for the Cuban peasants.
** Located in the eastern half of the island, Guáimaro was the political center of the *mambí* rebellion.
*** The Ten Years War began when the Cuban leader Carlos Manuel de Céspedes proclaimed Cuba's independence at the town of Yara on October 10, 1868.

were the true victims of the inequality and discrimination embodied in the oppressive feudal regime maintained by Spain in her colony.

After thirty years of struggle, the Cuban people ended Spanish domination but did not thereby gain true independence. The newborn republic came to be a semicolony of the powerful northern neighbor which imposed on it the Platt Amendment. The situation of the working masses did not essentially change, much less that of women and Blacks, who were cruelly discriminated against by the socioeconomic system.

The capitalist regime that was outlined under the colonial regime and fleshed out under the republic could not attain its full development because this was impeded by the domination of North American imperialism. The imperialists took control of the island's best lands, invested great sums in the sugar industry, and made Cuba a backward one-crop country with little industrial development. The Cuban people, whose rulers subordinated themselves to foreign interests, suffered the most brutal exploitation.

The scarcity of work gave rise to unemployment, with thousands of heads of households working only part of the year or sporadically, receiving the most miserable wages. Women were obliged to augment the scanty family budget. In doing so, they carried out tasks at home that permitted them to earn a few cents, without ceasing to attend to the domestic tasks—staying up late at night tied to the sewing machine or the ironing table, working hard to alleviate their family's agonizing life.

Only on rare occasions were the doors of industry opened to women, generally in the textile and tobacco industries, where the bosses saw them as cheap labor, forcing them to work inhumanly long hours in unsanitary conditions, without any protection by the law.

The situation of peasant women was even more desperate. The latifundists stripped the *guajiros* of their land and submerged them in the most appalling misery. In order to subsist it was necessary for the whole family, including small children, to engage in hard labor.

Women helped with the planting, the harvesting, and tending the animals. Lacking the most elementary living conditions, they inhabited dirt-floor *bohios,** surrounded by starving and bare-

* Huts inhabited by the Cuban peasantry.

footed children suffering from parasites, and they carried out the most exhausting work.

This brutal exploitation caused an exodus from the rural areas. Entire families headed for the city in search of better opportunities for work—which, of course, they never found. Peasant women thus fell into being domestic servants, the most downtrodden sector, carrying out every day the most burdensome and humiliating tasks in exchange for a miserable wage.

And even worse was the situation of Black women, who suffered the double discrimination of sex and color. Having no access to office or retail-sales positions, they had to resort to the lowest-paying jobs: in industries harmful to health like tobacco, or as maids in the homes of wealthy families.

The misery produced by lack of work threw thousands of women from the countryside and the city onto the torturous and denigrating road of prostitution.

The prejudices inherited from the feudal system of colonial Cuba, and continued under the semicolonial and semifeudal regime of the republic, even discriminated against rich and middle-class women, keeping them out of professional jobs. (Only teaching was considered a proper career for a woman.) Especially in the early years of the republic, women were neither admitted into public administration nor did they participate in the country's political life.

Starting from the vantage point of feminism, women began to demand their right to suffrage, protection on the job, and legal and economic equality with men.

In order to raise these demands, the First National Congress of Women was organized in 1923, at which there was a total absence of workers, peasants, and Blacks. However, the feminists raised the problem from the false angle of women against men, and they did not focus it as a fight of women together with men against the socioeconomic oppressor, which is the working-class point of view.

It was in the decade of the 1930s when women were massively incorporated into the struggle for national liberation. The precarious economic situation which Cuba was going through at the time owing to the deep crisis which the sugar industry had been suffering for years, plunged the working masses into the most terrifying misery, with unemployment reaching alarming figures. Professionals and small proprietors were also harshly affected.

Strike waves followed, culminating in the general strike of August 1933, which brought about the fall of the tyrannical government of Machado but which did not succeed in eliminating the imperialist domination of our country's economic and political life.

Women participated in the vanguard of these struggles and, as a consequence, won the right to vote in 1934. They also gained a better consciousness of their position in society.

Fighting all injustices and discrimination, the working class, and especially its Marxist-Leninist vanguard, took up the banner of women's rights, understanding that this struggle was part of the general fight against the social system responsible for discrimination. And as a result, in the constitution of 1940 the principle of equal pay for equal work was consecrated, discrimination for reasons of sex was declared illegal and punishable by law, full civil rights were granted to married women, and maternity protection for working women was regulated.

The legal recognition of these rights undoubtedly constituted the first step toward the liberation of women. But in practice the law was not carried out. "Equality before the law is not equality in life," said Lenin. In point of fact, the constitution of 1940 did not change women's position of inferiority. In practice women received inferior wages to those of men and were denied access to better-paying and more responsible jobs. The laws on maternity, retirement, vacations, etc., were not complied with.

This situation could be seen concretely in the case of the female textile workers, especially in the clothes-making branch of the industry, where the work was almost completely done by women. These workers were paid low wages, since those from the city were supposed to be earning a daily minimum of $3.30, and those from the countryside were supposed to be paid $3.10, yet they were paid only $1.50 a day. They had to work more than eight hours, and to get around the social security laws only half of the employees were listed on the books. It is important to point out that in the Ariguanabo textile factory no women were admitted after 1940 so that the employers would not have to comply with the constitutional provisions that favored women.

In spite of the fact that racial discrimination was considered illegal, employment practices continued being as discriminatory as they had been previously.

And what can we say about the peasant woman? She continued living under the enslaving yoke of the *bohío* without any hope of liberation. The agrarian reform promised by the constitution was not put into effect by the corrupt politicians, who were only concerned with getting votes in order to defend the interests of the exploiting classes and to satisfy their own petty aspirations.

With Batista's coup in 1952, a brutal and bloody tyranny began, which, hardly on being established, provoked the furious rebellion of the most valiant elements of the population. The assault on Moncada, the audacious action by a group of valiant young people, aroused our people for a heroic armed struggle against the tyranny—a fight that continued the traditions of the freedom struggles of 1868, 1895, and 1933.

Women were present during the first outbreak of the struggle. They also participated, actively and responsibly, in the war that the Cuban people, led by Fidel Castro, waged in the Sierra Maestra against Batista's dictatorial government that was subservient to imperialism.

During that unforgettable stage, women together with men participated in the two currents of the struggle—in the armed insurrection and in the underground—giving immense demonstrations of valor, self-sacrifice, and patriotism. Among the martyrs of the struggle were Lidia and Clodomira.* Lidia was quiet, modest, and tenacious. Clodomira, astute and talkative, with a limitless audacity. Both of them continue to live in the hearts of the people.

Throughout this difficult process, women many times took up vanguard positions; carrying out formidable mass actions, protest demonstrations, strikes; making unheard-of efforts to obtain the unity of all the opposition forces in common action against the tyranny.

On that glorious January 1, 1959, Cuba achieved the destruction of the semicolonial and latifundist regime. The hopes of a people, embodied in more than a century of struggle for their liberty, became a reality.

*   *   *

When the revolution came to power there were tens of thousands of prostitutes, hundreds of thousands of illiterate women, 70,000 domestic servants. Gambling was a big business, vice and corruption were encouraged, and the population was denied its most elementary rights: access to education, to medical care, to hospitals, to recreation. All that was reserved for the privileged classes alone.

Our women, as was true of our people in general, lacked an

* Lidia Doce and Clodomira Ferrals Acosta were Rebel Army messengers captured and tortured to death by Batista's army.

adequate ideological and cultural level. But, as with the rest of the people, they expressed their rejection of the dictatorship that tried to drown the growing popular rebellion in blood, that unleashed a ferocious repression, and that murdered our best sons and daughters while trying to rob our nation of its last vestige of dignity and fighting spirit.

How many mothers lost their sons and daughters? Twenty thousand martyrs gave their lives to make Cuba the first free territory in America!

That's why Cuban women joyously and enthusiastically came out to cheer the march of the victorious Rebel Army through towns and cities on that glorious day in January 1959. It was an army of peasants and workers symbolizing the revolutionary victory and the end of more than a half century of pain.

What did the triumphant revolution offer our women? A new life, filled with possibilities and prospects, in which their deepest dreams might become reality. A society in which that which is most precious to us all—our children's future—would be assured. A different society, where the people would be masters and mistresses of their own destiny, where they would exert their rights fully, where new values would come into being. The triumph offered our women the opportunity to study and to work, it offered them economic security, thereby putting an end to oppression and hardship. It opened prospects of health care, of social security. For women, the revolution meant the opportunity to attain human dignity.

At the triumph of our revolution there were women's groups of a social nature in our country, and others that belonged to different political movements. Throughout the first months of 1959 new groups appeared, in support of the different revolutionary laws or coming out for women's rights.

In an effort to bring the voice of our women—revolutionary women from the first free territory in America—to our sisters throughout the continent, the Cuban Commission for the First Latin American Congress of Women was set up with many of the existing organizations represented.*

After this congress, it was important to continue strengthening the new organization of women, whose goal was to push the revolution forward and to implement the resolutions taken at the

*This congress was held in Chile in November 1959, sponsored by the Women's International Democratic Federation. A delegation of seventy-six attended from Cuba.

Chilean event. At first our grouping was called the Congress of Cuban Women for the Liberation of Latin America. By August 23, 1960, with nearly 70,000 women integrated into revolutionary tasks, the single, all-encompassing women's organization was founded and Fidel provided the name: Federation of Cuban Women.

Those were the first steps, steps which established unity, got the women's organization off the ground, and gave women a consciousness of their force in numbers.

The revolutionary government had already begun the process of radically transforming our country's economic, political, and social structure. The Agrarian Reform Law had been passed as well as the nationalization of the country's sugar mills, the Urban Reform Law, the nationalization of banks, foreign industry, and capital.

Women were firm in their support of these laws that granted the people the benefits of their own wealth, a wealth which for so long had been plundered by the capitalists. The clash with imperialism was to become even sharper with the passage of these measures. From the very triumph of the revolution, we began to feel imperialism's aggressions and threats. Women, along with all our people, demanded the right to prepare themselves to be useful in defending their homeland.

Everyone's contribution was necessary. We had to organize and train the enthusiastic, firm, and powerful mass that our women made up. Thus the importance of our work aimed at winning over more and more women, uniting them, and with them, building a conscious force for the cause of the revolution.

The federation initiated first-aid courses. Through our work at the delegation level we incorporated tens of thousands of comrades into the National Revolutionary Militia.

The organization put all its efforts into raising the ideological, political, and cultural level of our women, in order to obtain, in the shortest possible time, their incorporation, their participation in the great tasks our country was already carrying out.

We had to change women's mentality—accustomed as they were to playing a secondary role in society. Our women had endured years of discrimination. We had to show her her own possibilities, her ability to do all kinds of work. We had to make her feel the urgent needs of our revolution in the construction of a new life. We had to change both woman's image of herself and society's image of women.

We started our work by means of simple tasks that allowed us to reach out to women, to get them out of the narrow, limited framework they moved in. To explain the revolution's purpose to them, and the part they would have to play in the process.

From the very beginning, we pursued a double goal:

• to raise consciousness through ideological education, so that new tasks could be performed;

• to raise the ideological level through the tasks themselves.

There was an intimate relationship between the work and the ideological education.

Simple dressmaking classes provided an efficient way to bring women together. Their interest in learning how to cut and sew in many cases prompted them to take their first steps outside the home. Once inside the classrooms, we gave them lectures on cultural and political improvement. First-aid courses also served this same purpose. Thousands of women enrolled in these courses, anxious to be of use in the face of imperialist aggression.

Voluntary work opened new prospects for many women who wanted to contribute to the process. Many participated enthusiastically in the first people's *zafra*,* and in the cotton, coffee, and other harvests.

Many of these women engaged in productive activity for the first time. Voluntary work was beginning to fulfill its purpose: opening new horizons for women, showing them it was possible to take part, creating a new consciousness.

In the rural areas we had started organizing peasant women from the very beginning. Delegations were set up throughout the Cuban countryside, the literacy campaign was begun, courses were given in cutting, sewing, crafts. Every activity initiated in the cities was duplicated in the rural zones. Later, when the National Association of Small Farmers was founded, we began a joint program aimed at increasing our work with women at every peasant base.

Throughout 1959 and 1960 the counterrevolution—organized, financed, and directed from the United States—was relentlessly trying to defeat the consolidation of our people's power. With their notorious methods, they unleashed a campaign of slander, rumors, sabotage, and other types of aggression in an effort to spread panic and hold back this process we had initiated. But our people confronted the enemy categorically, determined to continue on the path we had chosen.

From the start, the FMC organized and oriented its members

*sugar harvest

to keep on the offensive. We helped to destroy the enemy's campaign of lies and showed our determination to defeat the counterrevolution on all fronts.

Those were years of constant mobilization, combating the counterrevolution's criminal actions in all areas. Many churches became arms caches and the bourgeoisie often launched demonstrations that had their beginnings in these "places of worship." The firm action of our revolutionary women was central to checking these counterrevolutionary manifestations. We forced them to retreat; we showed them the irreversible force of people in power. Among the members of the FMC who stood up to the counterrevolutionaries were many honest Christian believers who were alert to all the enemy's tricks.

When Fidel appealed to the people to create the Committees for the Defense of the Revolution—a well-aimed blow at the counter-revolution—the federation oriented its ranks to contribute in every way possible to organizing a committee on every block.

Nineteen-sixty-one was a year of great historic importance in our revolutionary process.

On April 16 of that year, before an armed people and during the funeral eulogy for those who fell in the attack that preceded the Bay of Pigs aggression, Fidel declared the socialist nature of our revoluton.

The Bay of Pigs went down in history as imperialism's first defeat on the continent. We all took up arms against the aggressor.

The federation worked on all fronts to fully carry out every mission entrusted to it. The Sanitary Brigadistas working under the bombs at Ciudad Libertad became the seed of the future Auxiliary Corps of the Revolutionary Armed Forces Medical Service.

On the front lines, women from the FMC helped bring supplies to the first-aid posts, managed one hundred kitchens and three hospitals—where wounded fighters were taken—and all over the country the federation mobilized women to replace militiamen who went into combat. FMC women also participated in the collection of clothing, medicine, and food.

Thousands of women went to donate blood, enrolled in the militia, came to join the organization. Fear was not a part of those days. Implacable hatred of the enemy shone in our eyes, tightened our fist, and encouraged us to keep on fighting.

An FMC members from Las Villas gives us this testimony: ". . . We arrived in Junquito in our car weighted down with food, and when we got to kilometer number 3 they wouldn't let us through. When they withdrew from San Blas we got as far as the Muñoz Canal. Once Girón was ours again, we were there with our little food-carrying car and with aid for our troops. When Comrade Fidel arrived at the place where the tank troops were concentrated he ordered the infantry to advance, and he was on top of one of those tanks moving towards the enemy. We see Fidel—and our commander-in-chief gave us of the federation the responsibility of delivering food and medicine to the captured mercenaries before giving them to our own troops. This was a task we were very careful to carry out exactly as ordered. In fact, it was carried out with special care."

And everywhere, in every town and city, members of the federation and members of the Committees for the Defense of the Revolution kept up a permanent guard to prevent the internal enemy from starting a single action against the revolution.

And so, men and women prepared themselves, not only to handle weapons, first aid, evacuation, and other wartime support actions, but also to keep production at its usual level. We did not allow even a momentary stoppage on any front.

Let us remember the firm attitude of our mothers, the mothers of the youngsters—girls as well as boys—who were at that moment carrying out the literacy campaign all over our national territory. They were fulfilling a historic mission and they didn't falter. Neither did our peasant women, who, as the attack was launched, were on their way to Havana to enroll in the first dressmaking course. They didn't hesitate for one moment.

During the Bay of Pigs attack, women also gave their lives. Fe del Valle, a leader of the federation at her workplace, met her death in the criminal sabotage fire which consumed the El Encanto department store.

Cira María García, secretary general of the FMC at the Bay of Pigs, and Juliana Montano, an FMC member, fell under the bullets of the mercenary invaders. And so a working woman and two peasants joined the glorious ranks of those who offered their lives in that heroic saga.

What a lesson of determination and patriotism our people gave during those days of April 1961!

And how determined our women were to defend the socialist and democratic revolution of the humble and for the humble, as Fidel proclaimed on that April 16!

Not only at the Bay of Pigs did women show their revolutionary fervor. Later, through the dramatic days of the October Missile Crisis, when our homeland was on the verge of being wiped from the face of the earth, when in many parts of the world panic was the watchword; Cuban women, facing the possibility of nuclear war, calm and with dignity, occupied their places, ready to do their duty to the end.

Once more they would give proof of their courage and self-sacrifice when Hurricane Flora leveled everything in its path and the federation took part in the evacuation of the disaster areas, in the organization of aid for the injured, and in the operation of the shelters.* And when the cyclone had finished, these same women participated in reconstruction and in the planting and harvesting of coffee and other crops which had been affected.

There are many stories about how the FMC women worked during those days. Their work was constant.

And let's go back to 1961. That was the year the CIA financed, armed, and directed groups of bandits who succeeded in holing up for several months in different parts of the country, murdering our peasants and literacy workers, spreading terror, and sabotaging our economy.

In the Escambray area, the organization supported the activities of the Revolutionary Armed Forces and the militia, carrying out important tasks.

From February through May 1961, in the midst of the struggle against the bandits, we carried out our first antiparasite campaign in the Escambray mountains.

There are countless anecdotes that tell of women's courageous and heroic conduct in that struggle. A few months ago we received the following account from one of our women:

"We were ordered to join one of the batallions going where the bandits were. We had to march through Jíbaro, and our families were there to see us off. The lieutenant said: 'We will go through town single file and marching straight ahead. No goodbyes, and no looking to the side.' My children and I were at the front of the troop and right off we saw my mother, with the other mothers, waiting for us to pass. I stole a glance from the corner of my eye, and the boys did too, but we didn't say anything, and then (I still

---

*Hurricane Flora slammed into eastern Cuba in the fall of 1963, killing over a thousand people, destroying over 10,000 homes, and leaving a great deal of economic damage.

shiver when I think of it) she cried out to us: 'All right, my children, Patria o muerte!'* She didn't want us to have our last memory of her crying, so as not to effect us. . . ."

And we remember that other FMC member, in Palo Viejo, who on January 23, 1963, left her little girl in a corner of the barracks—and the barracks was being attacked by six bandits—and began to fill magazines and hand submachineguns and rifles to the three militiamen who, from the windows, fought fiercely for more than two hours.

In each one of the great tasks undertaken by the revolution, the federation has acted as a channel and catalyst for the masses of women, orienting women's efforts towards specific and necessary work.

*Homeland or- Death

Women in 1961: above, literacy drive; below, militia members

The Revolution Within the Revolution

Fidel Castro

The following is an excerpt from a speech given by Castro on December 9, 1966, at the closing of the Fifth National Plenary of the FMC held at Sandino Stadium in Santa Clara. It is reprinted from Granma Weekly Review, *December 18, 1966.*

Arriving here this evening, I commented to a comrade that this phenomenon of women's participation in the revolution was a revolution within a revolution. [*Applause*] And if we were asked what the most revolutionary thing is that the revolution is doing, we would answer that it is precisely this—the revolution that is occurring among the women of our country! [*Applause*]

If we were asked what things in the revolution have been most instructive for us, we would answer that one of the most interesting lessons for revolutionaries is that being offered by our women. [*Applause*]

You all know perfectly well that, in saying this, we are not uttering given words with intent to please the compañeras who are here tonight, but that we say it because it is what we firmly believe and feel.

But why is this one of the most interesting lessons? You yourselves may ask why. In reality, the most honest answer that we could give—and I assure you that the person who offers this answer is precisely one who has always believed himself free from prejudice—the answer is, I believe, that in reality all of us were prejudiced in regard to women. [*Applause*]

And if anyone had ever asked me if I considered myself prejudiced in regard to women, I would have said absolutely not, because I believed myself to be quite the opposite. I believed that an enormous potential force and extraordinary human resources for the revolution existed in our women.

But what has happened? What has occurred, or rather, what is occurring? We are finding that, in reality, this potential force is superior to anything that the most optimistic of us ever dreamed of. We say that perhaps at heart, unconsciously, something of a bias or underestimation existed.

For events are demonstrating, even now, the possibilities of women and the role that women can play in a revolutionary process in which society is liberating itself, above all, from exploitation, and from prejudices and a whole series of circumstances in which women were doubly exploited, doubly humiliated.

What have we found, for example, in regard to the work of women? I have been talking with several comrades and following my visit to the Banao Plan, [*Applause*] I told Comrade Milián: "I have the impression that the women working in this plan are more responsible and more disciplined than the men. [*Applause*] I have the impression that they will dedicate themselves to the work with more enthusiasm, more passion, more dedication."

And Milián—although I certainly don't want to give this comrade a bad name with the women of Las Villas—argued with me, "Well, but—really—the case of the young men who are in the Juraguá Plan of the Young Communists . . ."*

I told him that finding a spirit of discipline and enthusiasm for work in a program involving selected Young Communists was not as extraordinary as finding the same spirit of discipline and enthusiasm in a program carried out by women who had not been specially chosen for this program, who had not been chosen by an organization, but had simply volunteered to do this work. [*Applause*]

What have we found? What is being found everywhere in this revolutionary program, as far as the Cuban women are concerned? Well, we are finding a whole series of things such as those I mentioned before: a great sense of responsibility, great seriousness, great discipline and enthusiasm.

What have we found right here in the province of Las Villas? Well, let us take the Banao Plan, for example. This program was growing and needed a cadre. Comrade Milián sought a cadre from the party—Comrade Santiago Acosta, from the Santo Domingo zone, I believe—and sent him to the Banao Plan as administrator.

But one day, Comrades Santiago Acosta and Rena Acosta—the specialist on technical matters—had to go abroad. They were the men holding the positions of greatest responsibility in the plan.

---

*Banao and Juraguá were agricultural areas undergoing development.

Someone had to be appointed to take their place and we decided to appoint Comrade Osoria, who was representing the Federation of Cuban Women on the directing board of the plan. [*Applause*]

This was the first time that responsibility for a program of this kind had been assigned to a woman. And what was the result? The comrades who had gone abroad returned; the party was faced by several problems in the zone of Sancti Spíritus. A cadre was needed to strengthen the party's work there so it was decided to transfer Comrade Santiago Acosta to Sancti Spíritus and leave Comrade Osoria as administrator of the Banao Plan. [*Applause*]

We firmly believe that this may some day even have historic significance, for it was the first time that a woman had been assigned to such a task, not for political reasons or to impress anyone, but simply because she had, objectively speaking, proved herself capable of heading such a program.

And from that moment on, we thought it would be reasonable and an excellent thing indeed to have a woman directing a plan involving thousands of women workers. [*Applause*]

Moreover, when it became necessary to organize the work brigades, a number of women who had distinguished themselves for their great spirit of work were chosen as brigade leaders.

This gave us an idea:

We had to train a group of technicians for this type of work and, at first, ten comrades from the Technological Institute had been sent here to specialize in this branch of agriculture. We decided that twenty additional students who were to be sent here to specialize in this field should be chosen from among the female students at the Technological Institute.

Thus, the workers, the brigade leaders, and the technicians— that is, the technical and administrative staff—is going to be made up almost entirely of women. Yes, women! [*Applause*]

This is one of the great lessons we spoke about before: one of the great lessons and perhaps one of the greatest victories over prejudices that have existed, not for decades or centuries but for thousands of years. We refer to the belief that all a woman could do was wash dishes, wash and iron clothes, cook, keep house, and bear children—[*Applause and exclamations*] age-old prejudices that placed women in an inferior position in society. In effect, she did not have a productive place in society.

Such prejudices are thousands of years old and have survived through various social systems. If we consider capitalism, women—that is, lower-class women—were doubly exploited or doubly humiliated. A poor woman, part of the working class or of a working-class family, was exploited simply because she was poor, because she was a member of the working class.

But in addition, although she was a woman of the working class, even her own class looked down on and underrated her. Not only was she underestimated, exploited, and looked down upon by the exploiting classes, but even within her own class she was the object of numerous prejudices.

So all these events have been a great lesson to all of us, to every revolutionary. Naturally, a considerable amount of prejudice still persists. If women were to believe that they have totally fulfilled their role as revolutionaries in society, they would be making a mistake. It seems to us that women must still fight and exert great efforts to attain the place that they should really hold in society.

If women in our country were doubly exploited, doubly humiliated in the past, then this simply means that women in a social revolution should be doubly revolutionary. [*Applause*]

And perhaps this is the explanation, or at least the social basis, for the resolute, enthusiastic, firm, and loyal support given by Cuban women to this revolution.

This revolution has really been two revolutions for women; it has meant a double liberation: as part of the exploited sector of the country, and second, as women, who were discriminated against not only as workers but also as women, in that society of exploitation.

The attitude of Cuban women toward the revolution corresponds to this reality; it corresponds to what the revolution has meant to them.

And the support of the popular masses for the revolution is directly proportional to what the revolution has meant to them in terms of their liberation.

There are two sectors in this country, two sectors of society which, aside from economic reasons, have had other motives for sympathizing and feeling enthusiasm for the revolution. These two sectors are the Black population of Cuba and the female population.

I suppose you recall that in Cuba's old bourgeois constitution, there was an article which declared illegal any discrimination for reasons of race or sex. The constitution declared such discrimination illegal. But a constitution in a capitalist society, or such an article in a capitalist society, solves nothing, because discrimination for reasons of race and for reasons of sex existed in practice. And the basis for all of this was the existence of a class society which practiced exploitation.

In a class society, which is to say, a society of exploiters and exploited, there was no way of eliminating discrimination for reasons of race or sex. Now the problem of such discrimination has disappeared from our country, because the basis for these two types of discrimination which is, quite simply the exploitation of man by man, has disappeared. [*Applause*]

Much news reaches us from the United States, for example, about the civil rights struggle of Blacks. Nevertheless, racial discrimination in the United States will not disappear until capitalist society has disappeared.

That is, discrimination will never be wiped out within the framework of capitalist society. Discrimination with respect to race and sex can only be wiped out through a socialist revolution, which eradicates the exploitation of man by man. [*Applause*]

Now, does the disappearance of the exploitation of man by man mean that all the conditions are immediately created whereby woman may elevate her position in society? No. The conditions for the liberation of women, for the full development of women in society, for an authentic equality of rights, or for authentic equality of women with men in society, require a material base; they require the material foundations of economic and social development.

I described before the opinion held by many men concerning the functions of women, and I said that among the functions considered to belong to women was—almost exclusively—that of having children. Naturally, reproduction is one of the most important of women's functions in human society, in any kind of human society.

But it is precisely this function, relegated by nature to women, which has enslaved them to a series of chores within the home.

There is a sign here in front of us, for example, which says, "One million women working in production by 1970." Unfortunately, it will not be possible to have one million working in production by 1970. We feel that this goal may be reached, perhaps, within ten years but not within four.

We could propose it as a goal to be reached by 1975. Why can't this goal be reached in four years? Because in order to have one million women working in production, we must have thousands of children's day nurseries, thousands of primary boarding schools, thousands of school dining halls, thousands of workers' dining halls; thousands of centers of social services of this type must be set up, because if not, who is going to cook for the second- or third-grade child when he comes home for lunch?

Who is going to care for unweaned infants, or babies of two, three, and four years of age? Who is going to prepare dinner for the man when he comes home from work? Who is going to wash, clean, all of those things? [*Applause*]

In other words, in order to reach the social goal of liberating women from all these activities that enslave her and impede her from full incorporation into work outside the home and all these activities she can engage in society, it is necessary to create the necessary material base, to attain the necessary social development.

It is impossible to construct the required thousands of children's day nurseries, school dining halls, laundries, workers' dining halls, boarding schools, in four years. In fact, merely to meet present needs, great effort is necessary on all fronts.

Everywhere women are working it has been necessary to make a special effort to establish day nurseries, set up boarding schools and all of the necessary institutions so that these women could be free to work.

At this stage of scarcity of cement, machinery, and construction equipment, the problem can be solved only through maximum efforts on all fronts: sometimes at a regional level, other times at a provincial or national level, using the resources we have at hand.

Nor can we expect the day nurseries to be perfect, the constructions to be perfect, nor the service. They must be as good as possible, but they cannot be perfect.

These problems will have to be solved in many areas of the country, little by little. One million women cannot be employed in one day. A whole series of economic steps must be taken, and agricultural plans set in motion.

It would be interesting to know how many women have already started to work in the production of consumer goods as well as in services since the triumph of the revolution, how many are working as nurses' aides, technicians, industrial and agricultural workers. If a statistical study were made as to how many women have begun to work since the triumph of the revolution, the number would probably be close to 150,000, and certainly no less than that! [*Applause*]

This figure, of course, is not based on exact statistics, and it seems to us that a study should be made in order to learn precisely how many women have found work in newly created jobs, in jobs created by the revolution.

Next year the number of women working will be considerably greater. Why? Because a whole series of plans will get underway, mainly in agriculture. Several thousand women are to be incorporated into the Banao Plan and when that plan reaches its maximum development, it will require six or seven thousand women.

In Pinares de Mayarí, some eight thousand women will be working by springtime. In the coffee-plant nurseries set up for the 1967-68 coffee-growing plan, 30,000 women will be needed and many thousands will work in the reforestation plans, in vegetable cultivation, and other thousands are being incorporated into jobs in the cities.

This means that more than 50,000 women will be involved in tasks related to production by next year, and this will require an enormous and simultaneous effort to be made so that all of the problems related to dining halls, schools, and children's day nurseries may be worked out.

I am going to tell you something. Without the incorporation of women, the Banao Plan could never have gotten off the ground, nor could the plans for microclimate vegetable cultivation in Oriente Province have been carried out. Without the incorporation of women, the plans for coffee growing could not even have been considered.

Many of the plans that the revolution is today drawing up and beginning to carry out could not have been conceived until the great reservoir of human resources that our society possesses in its women was clearly seen for what it was.

These plans, which stand for extraordinary contributions to the economic development of our country, to the increased well-being of our people, could not have been conceived without the mass incorporation of women into the work force.

The Struggle for Women's Equality

Fidel Castro

The FMC's Second Congress was held November 25-29, 1974. The following is the major part of the speech Castro gave at its conclusion. The text is from Granma Weekly Review, *December 8, 1974.*

Dear guests;
Dear comrades of the party and the government;
Dear comrades of the Federation of Cuban Women:

We have reached the end of this beautiful congress. And it is not easy to sum up an event so filled with accomplishments and hope.

In the first place it has not been entirely our congress; we have shared it amply with a worthy and representative delegation of the revolutionary women of the entire world.

The presence at this congress of such prestigious comrades as Fanny Edelmann, Valentina Tereshkova, Angela Davis, Hortensia Bussi; the presence of numerous women from the fraternal countries of Latin America; the presence of the Arab women, and especially the delegation of the heroic Palestinian people; the presence of the women of Indochina and among them, of the thousand-times heroic Vietnamese people; [*Applause*] of the Korean women, of the women of the revolutionary and progressive peoples of Africa, of the women from our sister socialist countries, and the representation of the working women of Western Europe; doesn't this tell us that the representatives of the noblest and most just causes in the whole world have gathered here?

Across oceans, boundaries, languages, the representatives of the progressive women of the entire world have joined hands at this congress. And there is no need to use the term "foreigner" to characterize these delegations, because at all times we have experienced the feeling that we are part of the same homeland, of the same people: the universal homeland, the human population.

This proves that nothing except exploitation and injustice separates people, and nothing unites people more than the community of ideals and the aspiration to justice.

The topics that we have been discussing at this congress have a truly universal interest. They are not just the problems of Cuban women but the problems of the vast majority of women in the world.

It is clear that women need to participate in the struggle against exploitation, against imperialism, colonialism, neocolonialism, racism; in a word: in the struggle for national liberation. But when the objective of national liberation is finally achieved, women must continue struggling for their own liberation within human society. [*Applause*]

We have brought along some data from a report made by the United Nations Department of Statistics that reveals women's situation in most of the world.

Women represent 34 percent of the work force, that is, 515 million workers. By the end of the present decade, it is estimated that this figure will rise to 600 million, and in the year 2000, to 842 million.

In Western Europe and North America, women constitute between 30 percent and 40 percent of the work force.

In spite of the increasing number of women in the ranks of the employed, particularly in professional and technical posts, the United Nations report points out that they are underpaid in comparison to men.

"Although it is true," says the report, "that the legal barriers against equal job opportunities for women are few and the principle of equal pay for equal work is now universally accepted, in practice the situation demands the urgent application of measures to eliminate such discrimination."

In many industrialized countries, women's wages are approximately 50 percent to 80 percent of men's for the same hours of work. In the developing nations, the low salaries for women indicate that women are engaged in the lowest levels of work and jobs in terms of skill and pay.

In general, this report refers to the question of wages. Of course, it does not analyze the infinite number of problems that affect women in the class society of the capitalist world.

Naturally, in the socialist countries women have advanced a long distance along the road of their liberation. But if we ask ourselves about our own situation: we who are a socialist country with almost sixteen years of revolution, can we really say that the Cuban women have acquired full equality of rights in practice, and that they are absolutely integrated into Cuban society?

We can analyze certain data. For example, before the revolution there were 194,000 working women. Of them, according to a report read here, 70 percent were domestics. Today we have three times more women working. The figure for women in civilian state jobs, which as you know include the majority of productive activities, services, and administration, is 590,000 women out of a total of 2,331,000 persons working. That is, 25.3 percent of the workers are women. Nevertheless, the number of women holding leadership posts in all this apparatus of production, services, and administration, is only 15 percent. Only 12.79 percent of our party members are women. A notably low figure. And the number of women who work as party cadres and officials is only 6 percent.

But we have an example that is still more illustrative and is related to the elections held for People's Power in the province of Matanzas. The number of women selected as candidates was 7.6 percent and the number of women elected was 3 percent, to which the comrade from Matanzas referred.

The figures are really something to be concerned about, to make us do something about this problem. Because in those elections the candidates were proposed by the masses, and the masses only proposed 7.6 percent women candidates, when women make up approximately 50 percent of the population. Only 3 percent of those elected by the masses were women.

Who here at this congress, what invited delegate who has been here with you for a week can understand, imagine, or conceive how, with such a strong and such a politically advanced women's movement, only 3 percent women were chosen in elections?

And these figures reflect nothing more than the reality that after more than fifteen years of revolution, we are still politically and culturally behind in this area.

The reality is that there are still objective and subjective factors that discriminate against women.

Naturally, if we compare our present situation with what existed before the revolution, the advances are enormous. It isn't even possible to make any kind of comparison between women's situation before the revolution and their present situation. And the situation which the revolution encountered fully justified the creation of the Federation of Cuban Women. Because our experience teaches us that when an underdeveloped country such as ours liberates itself and begins to construct socialism, a mass organization like this one is necessary, since women have innumerable tasks to face up to within the revolutionary process. And for this reason we believe that the decision to develop this women's movement, to create this organization that was born on August 23, 1960, was really a wise decision because the work this organization has done could not have been carried forward by any other means.

What would the party have done without this organization of women? What would the revolution have done?

It is true that we have other magnificent mass organizations, such as the trade unions, the CDRs, the peasant organizations, the youth and student organizations, the Pioneers, and even the organization of the day-care centers. But what organization could have fulfilled the tasks that the Federation of Cuban Women has accomplished?

Comrade Vilma gave a significant historical account of those innumerable tasks, but it is sufficient to recall, first of all, the struggle to develop culture and political understanding in Cuban women, because in capitalist society women really remain culturally and politically downtrodden, they have even fewer educational opportunities than men, and many times women in class society are deceived precisely because of that low political level and are frequently used against revolutionary processes.

It is enough to recall that among those tasks were some of great importance. In the first place, the tasks related to the defense of the revolution and the homeland, the struggle against illiteracy, the struggle for the education of the daughters of peasants, the struggle in preparing domestics for doing productive jobs, the struggle against prostitution, the struggle to incorporate women into the work force, the struggle to create day-care centers, the tasks of support for education, the public health campaigns, the social work, the deepening of political and ideological consciousness among women, and the struggle for the development of an internationalist spirit in Cuban women.

The federation has worked in all those fields and has successfully completed all its tasks. And only the women themselves could have carried out those activities with such efficiency.

But now, in this present stage of the revolution, women have a basic task, a historical battle to wage.

And what is that task? What is that battle? Could you give the answer?

What was the crux, the center of the analysis and the efforts of this congress? The struggle for women's equality. [*Applause*] The struggle for the full integration of Cuban women into society!

And that is really a historical battle. And we believe that this objective is precisely the focal point of this congress, because, in practice, women's full equality still does not exist. [*Applause*]

And we revolutionaries must understand this, and women themselves must understand it. It is not, of course, only a task for women. It is a task for the whole society! [*Applause*]

But no one need be frightened because women's equality in society is being discussed, although some were frightened when the discussion of the Family Code draft was launched. [*Laughter and applause*] And Blas [Roca] explained to us here the many conversations he has had with certain male comrades who didn't understand, and he summed up his ideas with a beautiful argument that man's happiness was not possible without woman's happiness. [*Applause*]

And we don't see why anyone should be frightened, because what should really frighten us as revolutionaries is that we have to admit the reality that women still do not have absolute equality in Cuban society. [*Applause*]

What must concern us as revolutionaries is that the work of the revolution is not yet complete.

Of course, in this lack of equality, in this lack of full integration, as I said, there are objective factors and there are subjective factors. Naturally, everything that prevents the incorporation of women into the work force makes this process of integration difficult, makes this process of achieving full equality difficult. And you have seen that precisely when women are incorporated into the work force, when women stop performing the traditional and historical activities, is when these problems begin to show up.

In conversations with some of the delegates to this congress, they expressed their great satisfaction and joy that during these days of the congress, many of their husbands had remained at home taking care of the children so they could come to the congress. [*Applause*] It is unquestionable that if those women had not been integrated into the federation and had not carried out this work, if they had not been revolutionary militants and had not been participating in this congress, such a problem never would have arisen in their homes, and the opportunity for those husbands to become aware of such a necessity and of such duties would never even have existed.

Among the objective factors that still hinder women's incorporation into the educational system and the work force, some were pointed out here, such as the lack of sufficient day-care centers, of sufficient semiboarding schools,* of sufficient boarding schools, problems concerning the hours in which the schools function; to which we can add such factors as the lack of sufficient jobs for women throughout the country and, of course, the fact that many women do not have the level of skill for productive work.

In this area, as far as the day-care centers and education are concerned, over and beyond the great efforts that the revolution has already made, during the next few years—and particularly in the next five years from '76 to '80—a still greater effort will be made, in the first place, to satisfy the growing educational needs of our people and at the same time to facilitate the incorporation of women into the work force.

The present capacity of day-care centers is approximately 50,000 children. In the first version of the next five-year plan, the idea of constructing 400 day-care centers with state brigades has been considered, apart from those the microbrigades construct,** [*Applause*] in order to increase the capacity up to 150,000 children. That is, three times the capacity we now have.

We are also proposing to construct 400 semiboarding schools for 300 pupils each, or the equivalent, in order to increase the capacity by 120,000 children; to construct no less than a thousand high schools with a capacity of more than a half million additional boarding school students.

Special attention will also be given to a type of school that you know is very important, the special schools for pupils with certain problems. The proposal is to build capacity for 40,000 new pupils in this type of special education.

At the same time, the revolution will continue developing the public health sector in the next few years: 49 new hospitals, 110 polyclinics, 19 dental clinics, 51 homes for the aged, and 16 homes for the disabled will be built throughout the country.

The total investment in education and public health in the next five years will be approximately 1.65 billion pesos. [*Applause*]

---

*Schools where lunches are served, enabling the children not to have to go home in the middle of the day. As of March 1980, 280,000 primary school children attended these types of schools.

**The microbrigades are a program to help ease Cuba's housing shortage by organizing brigades of workers from a workplace who are relieved of some of their normal responsibilities to build houses for themselves and others in their workplace. They have also built schools, nurseries, community buildings, shopping centers, polyclinics, and parks.

We believe this is good news for the members of the federation. [*Applause*] And it does not mean starting something new, but rather increasing the rhythm of what is now being built, because more than 180 high schools accommodating 500 students each are now being built per year. [*Applause*]

The hospital construction program is moving ahead; the first brigades for the construction of day-care centers have also been organized. And the brigades necessary to construct the 400 day-care centers that have been programmed and to construct the special schools, the polyclinics, the homes for the aged, for the disabled, and the semiboarding schools at the primary level—those brigades that are still lacking will be organized beginning in 1975.

This program is in progress and we are perfectly sure that it will be carried forward.

During the discussion we could appreciate the enormous importance that you attach to these problems and especially to the problems of education. It can be said that a large part of the discussion in the congress revolved around these questions. Yet in the fields of education and public health our country already occupies first place among all the countries of Latin America. [*Applause*]

And we are really just beginning. It is precisely in the last years that it has been possible to provide a great impulse to school construction. And there were not enough installations nor enough cadres, nor enough teachers. How many difficulties the revolution has had to confront in order to carry forward these educational programs and to carry forward the public health program, when out of the 6,000 doctors we had, almost all of them concentrated in the city of Havana, the Yankees took 3,000 from us. One of the many forms the imperialists use to carry out their crimes; because if in other places—as in Vietnam—they shell and bomb in order to kill people, here they tried to take away all the doctors so the people would die, [*Applause*] just as they blockaded us and still blockade us to try to starve our people to death.

Of course, today we already have 9,000 doctors, and they are magnificent doctors, [*Applause*] and more than 6,000 young people are studying in the schools of medicine. [*Applause*] So that not only are we able to satisfy our medical necessities, and do so with increasing quality, but we have also even been able to organize medical brigades to help other fraternal peoples. [*Applause*] And in the years to come we will graduate some 1,000 doctors each year, [*Applause*] and some of those doctors will be able to offer their internationalist services. [*Applause*] And our medical services will go on improving in quality and will go on conquering disease and will continue eradicating some of those diseases.

The minister of public health explained what the infant mortality rate is now: 27.4 per thousand live births. In Brazil—where there aren't even mortality statistics—it is estimated that it may be between 150 and 200. And unfortunately this is what takes place in many other Latin American countries. This means that for every infant that dies in Cuba, four, five, six, or seven infants die in other countries of Latin America. The same is true of many other problems: mortality at other ages—because we are talking about mortality in the first year of birth—medical care in general, education.

The minister of education explained the figures that reflect the progress of education in Cuba: all children enrolled in schools, the growing number of those graduating from the sixth grade, and the explosion we are already having at the high school level, with the result that all the construction we're building isn't enough.

But now in the years to come the problem will be not only the number of children studying, but also the quality of our education. And our education will improve in quality year by year with the new system that is being projected and with the growing number of young people studying to be teachers and joining the Pedagogical Detachment.*

So that if we now already occupy the very first place among Latin American countries in education and public health, what will it be in five or six more years? What will it be in future years, given this rhythm of construction, this rhythm of advancement we now have?

And this is the blockaded country, the country against which the imperialists have committed their crime of blockade. And we might ask ourselves: why the blockade? And what has happened in the countries they didn't blockade? What has happened in education? What has happened in public health? How many illiterates are there? How many children without schools? And

*The Pedagogical Detachments were formed to meet the shortage of teachers arising from the postrevolution "baby boom." They were composed of 16-year-old youth who received their training while teaching in the elementary schools.

how many children die each year for lack of food, medicine, medical treatment, and everything?

Then what did imperialism want for the peoples of Latin America? To maintain that situation! And what did they want for Cuba? To prevent us from doing what we are doing! And, it is true, they have achieved one objective, yes: keeping Latin America in that humiliating present situation. But on the other hand, with all their crimes and their blockades, they haven't been able to prevent the social successes of the Cuban revolution. [*Prolonged applause*]

And these truths, these realities, can no longer be hidden, no matter what desperate measures imperialism and its lackeys resort to. And these truths are beginning to become known throughout the world.

So our country can continue its march forward serenely and confidently. These fifteen years have not passed in vain. And the revolution is more secure today than it has ever been before, the revolution is more solid today than it has ever been before, and the revolution is advancing today at a rhythm it has never had before.

I have said all this, speaking of the objective factors that hinder the integration of women, referring to schools, hospitals, etc. And I really simply wanted to express to you the ideas and the projects related to the solution of these problems.

You come from all over the country. There are comrades here from Guane, from the Isle of Pines, from the province of Havana, from Matanzas, Jagüey, the Escambray, Sancti Spíritus, Sola, Veguitas, Guantánamo; [*Applause*] and you know how the revolution's schools are springing up all over, transforming the landscape and the life of our countryside. [*Applause*] And we will march forward at this rhythm.

The question has been raised here as to whether the same measures were being applied to the junior high schools in the countryside as to the semiboarding schools with respect to the children of working mothers, and actually there are some regions where all the pupils, all of them, are now in the junior high schools in the countryside, all the pupils of that level. There are various regions in the country where of course this problem no longer exists because all the young people are taken care of.

The minister of education explained the factors that hinder this, taking into consideration the objective of not having a single youth without a corresponding high school, not one sixth grade graduate who does not go on to a higher level; the same principle for the difficulties involved can be applied to these schools as well. But we believe that, even so, something can still be done to favor the children of working mothers, high school students, in certain regions, in certain provinces; because many times they take out a complete school in order to put a primary school there, for example, and they have to find locations for those pupils in any case.

But this proposal was a just proposal; that is the aspiration expressed here by some comrade delegates, and at the same time it is also only fair that the ministry's difficulties be taken into account since its number-one problem is to make all the changes and combinations possible in order to achieve the objective of having no sixth grade graduate left without a school.

We also believe that in the long run the question of auxiliary teachers will have to be solved. We believe that the country will have to face up to the necessity of employing a specific number of comrades in this task, and that it will be necessary to analyze the economic aspects and also the facilities that those auxiliary teachers must be given.

Given that there are presently close to 600,000 working women, and 250,000 more are to be incorporated in the next five years, there will be no other solution than to attack those problems related to the hour that the primary schools and the semiboarding schools begin to function, and the problems of Saturdays.

The question of vacations was also raised. And we believe that the country has the resources to deal with this problem of summer vacations, since we are building hundreds of junior high schools in the countryside, and those installations could also be used for vacation plans. They are magnificent installations, and we are analyzing the possibilities of using them during the summer for vacation plans.

Many of these problems that you have raised here can be solved with what we already have today. And in the long run, all these questions that hinder the incorporation of women into the work force—the most certain way for the advancement of Cuban women along the road of their own liberation; we will overcome all these objective difficulties sooner or later.

There are others that weren't mentioned, at least in the discussion at the congress, such as questions relating to laundries, etc., etc. But we will go on solving these material difficulties.

And now there remain the other difficulties we mentioned before: those of a subjective character. And what are those subjective difficulties? The problem of an old culture, of old habits, of old concepts, of old prejudices.

There are administrators, for example, who, whenever they can, will give a job to a man rather than to a woman, for a number of reasons: because they begin to think of problems of job slotting, of problems of maternity, of the difficulties of absenteeism a woman may have. The reasons, the factors, are many; but the fact is that women are discriminated against in terms of job opportunities.

One day, Resolution 47 was decreed, which froze a number of positions, certain positions, to be filled only by women. Later, that question was analyzed in the workers' congress and it was proposed that Resolution 47 be abolished, and at the same time, that Resolution 48, which prohibited women from taking certain jobs, be studied more deeply.

In any case, this problem must be attacked, if not in the form of freezing these jobs—which has raised certain difficulties, because many times the skilled female personnel for the job didn't turn up—at least in job slotting in workplaces, the positions in which women will be given preference must be noted; and in every new industry, every new workplace, these job slots must be noted. And the party, the workers' organizations, the mass organizations, and public administration, in judging the efficiency of those workplaces, must take into account whether the job slottings that give preference to women are really, in effect, occupied by women.

And in every new factory built in any Cuban town, it must now be indicated what work is to be given to women [*Applause*] so there will be time enough to proceed with the selection and training of those women.

The rules and policy of the party and of the mass organizations must be careful to maintain and ensure the conditions for women to be incorporated into the work force. First, it is a question of elemental justice; and second, it is an imperative necessity of the revolution, it is a demand of our economic development, because at some point, the male work force will not be enough, it simply will not be enough.

And for that reason it is necessary to wage a consistent battle against that mentality of discriminating against women in their job opportunities.

Here in the congress, you pointed out other types of difficulties women have, related to the home, related to child care, and related to old habits. And you suggested ways to overcome those difficulties.

In the investigation that was made, it was shown that there are attitudes held by men, negative attitudes, and that there are also negative attitudes held by some women, and that this requires a special educational effort.

We believe that this struggle against the discrimination of women, this struggle for women's equality and for women's integration, must be carried out by the whole society. And it is the task of our party, in the first place, and it is the task of our educational institutions and of all our mass organizations.

We were very pleased by the statements made here in the name of your youth, and how they committed themselves to wage the battle to overcome prejudices and the mentality that still exists. Perhaps these subjective factors imply an even greater struggle than the objective elements. Because with the development of our economy, we will overcome the material difficulties and one day we will have all the day-care centers we need, and we will have all the semiboarding schools we need, and all the boarding schools we need, and all the services we need. [*Applause*]

But we still have to ask ourselves when we will eradicate the age-old ways of thinking, when we will defeat all those prejudices. Of course, we have no doubt that those prejudices will be defeated. It also seemed very difficult to overcome the concepts on property that existed in our society before the revolution. It was impossible to conceive of life without private property. And today it really isn't possible to conceive of life without socialist ownership of the means of production. [*Applause*]

But many habits remain from the times when women were also property within society. And these ways of thinking have to be eradicated. And we understand that the Family Code itself, which has produced so much discussion, is an important legal and educational tool in helping to overcome those habits and those prejudices.

But in order to achieve those objectives women and men must struggle together, women and men have to become seriously and profoundly aware of the problem. They have to wage that battle together. And we are certain that it will be waged and that it will be won! And we believe that you are also certain of that!

[*Applause*] And the agreements of this congress will be magnificent tools in that struggle.

I believe that all the resolutions are very worthy and very important. The resolution on the working woman, on the young woman, the peasant woman, the housewife, and the role of the FMC, the role of the family in socialism; the special resolution on the participation of women in physical education, recreation, and sports; the resolution on International Women's Year, on solidarity, and the inspired appeal to Cuban, Latin American, and all women of the world, in solidarity with Chile—all these resolutions are resolutions worthy of this congress.

And we believe that all these documents must be taken up and studied. And studied not only by the federation, but also by the other mass organizations and by the party. [*Applause*] Because these resolutions represent a real program of work for this historical struggle, for this historical battle you have before you in order to fulfill this revolutionary duty.

One of the things that our revolution will be judged by in the future years is how we have solved women's problems in our society and in our homeland, [*Applause*] even though that is one of the revolution's problems that demands more tenacity, more firmness, more constancy, and more effort.

On the question of prejudice, we told you once what happened in the Sierra Maestra when we began to organize the Mariana Grajales Platoon, and the real resistance we encountered to the idea of arming that women's unit, which reminds us how much more backward we were a few years ago. Some men believed that women weren't capable of fighting.

But the unit was organized, and the women fought excellently, with all the bravery that the most valiant of our soldiers could have shown.

Nor was that the first time in history that this occurred. In the underground struggle women carried out an infinite number of tasks that, on occasion, placed them in greater danger than the dangers on the front line. And during World War II, during the fascist aggression against the Soviet Union, thousands of women fought in antiaircraft units, in fighter and bomber planes, and even with the guerrillas and at the front. But still the old prejudices seek to impose themselves.

Nature made woman physically weaker than man, but it did not make her morally and intellectually inferior to man. [*Applause*] And human society has the duty to prevent this difference in physical strength from becoming a cause for discrimination against women. This is precisely the duty of human society: to establish the norms of coexistence and justice for all.

Of course, the exploiting societies, the class societies, exploit women, discriminate against them, and make them victims of the system. Socialist society must eradicate every form of discrimination against women and every form of injustice and discrimination. [*Applause*]

But women also have other functions in society. Women are nature's workshop where life is formed. They are the creators par excellence of the human being. And I say this because, instead of being the object of discrimination and inequality, women deserve special consideration from society.

I mention this point because there is something that we must bear very much in mind: that the struggle for women's security and full integration into society must never be converted into lack of consideration for women: it never means the loss of habits of respect that every woman deserves. [*Applause*] Because there are some who confuse equality with rudeness. [*Applause*]

And if women are physically weaker, if women must be mothers, if on top of their social obligations, if on top of their work, they carry the weight of reproduction and child-bearing, of giving birth to every human being who enters the world, [*Applause*] and if they bear the physical and biological sacrifices that those functions bring with them, it is just that women should be given all the respect and all the consideration they deserve in society. [*Applause*]

If there is to be any privilege in human society, if there is to be any inequality in human society, there must be certain small privileges and certain small inequalities in favor of women. [*Applause*]

And I say this clearly and frankly, because there are some men who believe they're not obliged to give their seat on the bus to a pregnant woman, [*Applause*] or to an old woman, or to a little girl, or to a woman of any age who gets on the bus. [*Applause*] Just as I also understand it to be the obligation of any youth to give his seat on the bus to an old man. [*Applause*]

It is a question of the basic obligation we have toward others: on a bus, in productive work, on the truck, others always have to be given special consideration, for one reason or another.

It is true with women and must be so with women because they are physically weaker and because they have tasks and functions and human responsibilities that man does not have. [*Applause*]

For this reason we appeal to our teachers, we appeal to our

parents, we appeal to our youth organizations and our Pioneers to give special attention to this standard of conduct in children, to this standard of conduct in our youth.

Because it would be very sad if, with the revolution, there wasn't even the recollection of what certain men in bourgeois society did out of bourgeois or feudal chivalry. And instead of bourgeois and feudal chivalry, there must exist proletarian manners and proletarian consideration of women! [*Applause*]

And I say this with the certainty that the people understand it and share it, with the certainty that every mother and every father would like their son to be a chivalrous proletarian, [*Applause*] that type of man who is respectful of women and considerate of women, capable of making a small sacrifice that dishonors no man but on the contrary exalts and elevates him. [*Applause*]

And here, at the closing of this congress, in which the question of the struggle for women's equality and integration has become the center of Cuban women's political and revolutionary activity for future years, [*Applause*] I say this so that one thing isn't confused with the other. I am saying what I really feel.

And we constantly run up against even verbal, linguistic forms of discrimination against women. The comrade who spoke here in the name of the workers, Agapito Figueroa, spoke of the discriminatory terminology used. And we must be careful even about this. Because sometimes we use a slogan that seems very pretty, that says: "Woman must be man's comrade"; but one might also say: "Man must be woman's comrade." [*Applause*]

There is the linguistic habit of always making the man the center and this is inequality, it reflects habits of thinking, although language is the least important in the final analysis, words are the least important. There are times when words remind us of something in the past although they no longer have that meaning. Deeds are what are really important!

Many things about this congress have impressed us. As always, first of all, the enthusiasm, the joy, the interest you have shown; but very especially the political level this congress reflected, because this congress expressed the political development of Cuban women. The cadres that are rising in the Cuban women's movement impressed us; the mental sharpness, the depth, the security, and the conviction that the delegates to this congress reflected.

I know our guests were impressed because they saw the minister in discussions with you here and you in discussions with the minister; they were impressed by the great frankness, the great naturalness, the great spontaneity with which the debates evolved. And, all this, of course, in a very disciplined atmosphere.

We weren't really so impressed by those things because we are all accustomed to this, and there's nothing extraordinary in the fact that the minister or anyone else discusses matters with you, or discuss them in a student assembly or a workers' assembly or anywhere else; he discusses with the masses and, if necessary, gives the masses a thousand and one explanations. [*Applause*]

The revolution's force lies in this proximity, in this identification between the masses and the government, between the masses and the state, between the masses and authority. This is what gives the revolution an invincible force, because the masses see in everything—in the state, in the government—something that is theirs; not someone else's, not a foreign thing or a strange thing. And no leader can view positions, functions, authority as his own. [*Applause*] But in any case it has been highly flattering for us to see how our guests have commented about the form and character of the congress.

For me, the advances Cuban women have made are what impressed me, especially their present political culture and the values that are developing among the masses. It pleased me—and I am sure other comrades too—to see the magnificent leadership that has developed, the magnificent cadres directing this movement headed by Comrade Vilma Espín, [*Applause*] the very worthy leaders the organization has; their experience, their seriousness, their depth, along with their human qualities. And to see that in the provinces, in the regions, and in the municipalities, that type of cadre is arising, that type of leader is arising. And to see that the working masses sent such magnificent and brilliant delegates to this congress. [*Applause*]

We are gratified to see the force the revolution has in women; [*Applause*] we are gratified to confirm the revolutionary quality of Cuban women, [*Applause*] their self-sacrifice, discipline, and enthusiasm, their passion for the revolution, for just ideas, for the just cause of Cuban women, demonstrating their virtues which— as we have said on other occasions—are virtues demanded of the revolutionary militant and that women have to a very high degree. [*Applause*] And so we believe that our party must draw more from that force, [*Applause*] that our state must draw more from that force, [*Applause*] that our apparatus of production must draw more from that force. [*Applause*]

The revolution has in Cuban women today a true army,

[*Applause*] an impressive political force. [*Applause*] And that is why we say that the revolution is simply invincible. [*Applause*] Because when women acquire that level of political culture and revolutionary militancy it means that the country has made a very great political leap, that our people have developed extraordinarily, that our country's march toward the future can't be stopped by anyone. That things will only be better all the time, that things will only be superior all the time. And that is why the revolution is so strong; because of its mass organizations, because of the people's political consciousness, and because of its vanguard party. [*Applause*]

And every year that passes will be better. Every year that passes we will have a more educated, more aware, more revolutionary, and more internationalist people. [*Applause*]

So these are the impressions we take from this historical congress.

We think that you are also happy. [*Exclamations of "Yes!"*] that you are also satisfied, [*Exclamations of "Yes!"*] that you are proud of the congress. [*Exclamations of "Yes!"*] I can tell you that our party is also proud of the congress, is satisfied with the congress. [*Applause and songs*]

Sometimes you say that you have learned from us, but the reality is that we have learned much more from you, [*Applause*] we have learned much more from the people, from the masses. Because they always renew and fortify our confidence, our faith, our revolutionary enthusiasm. You help to educate us, and when I say us, I speak not only as leader of the party, I also speak as a man. [*Applause and slogans*] You help us all, all men, all revolutionaries, to have a clearer awareness of these problems. And you help the party and you help the leaders of the revolution: a party in which there is a very high percentage of men in the leadership, [*Laughter*] a government in which there is a very high percentage of men, so that it might seem to be a party of men and a state of men and a government of men. [*Laughter*] The day has to come when we have a party of men and women, [*Applause*] and a leadership of men and women, and a state of men and women, and a government of men and women. [*Applause*]

And I believe that all the comrades are aware that this is a necessity of the revolution, of society, and of history.

The great contemporary revolutionaries—Marx, Engels, Lenin—always understood the role of women.

Lenin said, and it has been repeated here several times, that the full victory of the people could not be achieved without the complete liberation of women.

And Martí, the apostle of our independence, had very high ideals and said very beautiful things about women; and not only beautiful but also profound and revolutionary. As when he said that the campaigns of the peoples are weak only when they do not enlist the heart of women; but when women move and help, when women stimulate and applaud, when educated and virtuous women anoint the work with the sweetness of their love, the work is invincible. [*Applause*] Or when he said that women's natural nourishment is the extraordinary. Or when he said that women, by instinct, divine the truth and precede it. Or when he stated that women will live as an equal of men, as a comrade, and not at their feet as a pretty toy. [*Applause*]

May we be worthy followers of the ideas of Marx, Engels, Lenin, and Martí. [*Applause*]

I know that your just aspirations and ideals, those of Cuban women, will penetrate deeply into the heart of revolutionaries and the heart of the entire people.

Patria o muerte! [Homeland or Death]

Venceremos! [We will win] [*Ovation*]

Cuban women in the work force

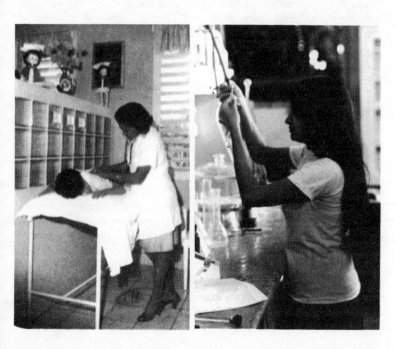

Thesis: On the Full Exercise
of Women's Equality

Communist Party of Cuba

*Formed in 1965 as a result of a fusion of the July 26 Movement,
the Popular Socialist Party, and the Revolutionary Directorate,
the Communist Party of Cuba is the political leadership that
directs the revolution's course. Composed initially of 45,000
members, it had grown to ten times that size by 1980, the
majority of them workers. In order to be accepted into party
membership, these workers have to be first nominated by their co-
workers on the job.*

*The Communist Party held its First Congress in December
1975. The congress took stock of the revolution's sixteen-year
history, laying down its principles and goals in a more complete
manner than had been done up to that time. A number of
different theses and resolutions were presented. One of the most
far-reaching was the* Thesis: On the Full Exercise of Women's
Equality. *The translation is by Michael Taber.*

Introduction

In closing the Second National Congress of the Federation of
Cuban Women, Commander Fidel Castro, first secretary of our
party, declared:

"What was the crux, the center of the analysis and the efforts
of this congress? The struggle for women's equality. The struggle
for the full integration of Cuban women into society!

"And that is really a historical battle. And we believe that this
objective is precisely the focal point of this congress, because in
practice, woman's full equality still does not exist."

In pointing to the historic nature of this battle, which concerns
all workers—men and women—and in which victory is indispensable for the proper construction of socialist society, Comrade
Fidel clearly stated the Marxist-Leninist principle that the
definitive solution to the problem involves: an uninterrupted

process of advancement in keeping with the country's economic development; the efforts of the socialist state; and the permanent ideological battle against the still-remaining prejudices and discrimination—a struggle which must be conducted both by the political, mass, and administrative organizations and bodies, and within the home itself, through the educational work of the family.

The success of this historic battle naturally presupposes, as required by communist morality, the extirpation down to its very roots of the holdovers of old attitudes toward women; the radical elimination of the prejudices and discrimination that still remain and wield a negative influence—the heritage of the centuries of humiliation experienced by women in societies based on exploitation—and which, in more than a few cases, hinder the full and effective exercise of the equality proclaimed by the revolution.

Thus, it is the task of the party and its members—at the same time that they foster the objective conditions for the growing integration of women into economic, social, and political life—to carry forward in all spheres of national life an ideological effort designed to eliminate the holdovers of the old society, seeing to it that all the people take part in this struggle.

I. Women's Contribution to Socialist Construction; Role of the Federation of Cuban Women

Women and the Revolution

Throughout the sixteen years that have gone by since the victory of the revolution, the situation of women has radically changed in accordance with the country's economic and political development and the ideas that are part and parcel of socialist society.

We have put behind us forever women's terrible plight under the bourgeois neocolonial republic, when they were subjected to a brutal and double exploitation, in conditions of humiliating dependency and legal submission to men, when their minimal formally established social rights were flouted. The future of working women, of peasant women, of the toiling families in general, held nothing but squalor, degradation, ignorance, and suffering. In the case of many women, it meant domestic service or prostitution. For almost all women, in keeping with the dominant bourgeois mentality, it meant being regarded as a decorative figure and sex object, whose place depended on class affiliation.

On January 1, 1959, the doors to a new life opened for Cuban women, who, from the very start, regarded as inalienably their own the revolutionary process that was beginning and to which they had made an important contribution.

Women have always taken part in each and every one of the struggles waged over a century of relentless fighting to win our homeland's freedom, independence, and sovereignty. From the glorious battles of the *mambí* army and the people's confrontations with the series of dictatorial regimes of the pseudorepublic, to the heroic actions of the Moncada Barracks and the Sierra Maestra and the underground struggle of that entire stage—on the front lines or in the rear, making a valuable contribution to bringing about the reality in which we live today.

Women, self-confident and sure of themselves, were part of the masses of people who, with irreversible determination after the victory of the revolutionary forces headed by Fidel, laid the groundwork for the definitive liquidation of neocolonialism, imperialist and bourgeois-latifundist exploitation, and for undertaking the conquest of the future. And then more than ever, women wanted to participate, to contribute to the creation of the new world that was coming into being, contributing their enthusiasm, their unconditional support, and their spirit of self-sacrifice.

Participation of Women in the Revolutionary Process

The revolution needed the contributions of everyone: men and women. It was absolutely vital to prepare the female population by helping them to sweep away centuries of backwardness and integrating them fully in the process that was beginning.

And so, the revolutionary leadership decided to found the Federation of Cuban Women, in order to educate women ideologically through each task, to create consciousness for undertaking increasingly complex tasks, to prepare women to take their place in the building of socialism, and to represent the specific interests and aspirations of this important sector of the population.

Hundreds of thousands of women throughout the country—in the city and the countryside—aware of the need for their contribution and spurred on by their willingness to contribute to economic and social progress, did not wait until all the material conditions were created. They joined in production, and in social and educational services, thereby embarking on the road to full liberation.

At present more than 600,000 women work in production or services, accounting for 25.3 percent of the country's labor force.

Each year an increasing number of women receive the National Heroine of Labor award.

Millions of women belong to the social and mass organizations, participate in the unions, in the CDRs, in the student federations. Women have been making a notable contribution in agricultural and industrial production, in construction and services, in social work, health care, the "mother-child health plans," education, the care and upkeep of social property, in the defense of the homeland and the revolution. They have contributed millions of hours of unpaid voluntary labor in as many activities as have been necessary for promoting the country's economic and social development plans.

Cuban housewives are no longer the women who traditionally lived only to take care of individual or family matters. Today they contribute their labor, their initiative, and their enthusiasm to the work of the revolution.

A deepgoing change has come about in the lives and consciousness of peasant women, who have consistently supported and continue to support the revolution: as members of the mountain militia, in voluntary labor, and in lending their warm support to the young members of the literacy brigades—to the teachers who worked with them in the great campaign against illiteracy.

Their selfless efforts in the FMC-ANAP Mutual Aid Brigades* have enabled many peasant women to attain the honor of being declared vanguard farmers.

Young women take an active part in all the fronts of the revolution, endowing each task with their enthusiasm and fervor in keeping with the lofty principles in which they have been educated. Today these women have the opportunity to study in schools or on the job, in the ranks of the Young Communist League [UJC] and in the student and mass organizations, learning to be useful to the revolution, to devote their best efforts to continuing the work of Moncada, and together with their companions, preparing to build the families that will live in socialist society.

A large number of women have served in the internationalist tasks that our people have undertaken in different parts of the world. And thousands of them have been selected to join the

---

*Begun in 1966, this joint effort between the FMC and the National Association of Small Farmers is designed to encourage peasant women to get involved in voluntary labor tasks.

worthy ranks of our party and the UJC because of their valuable contribution to the revolutionary process.

Role of the Federation of Cuban Women

In analyzing the impressive efforts and the active participation of women throughout these years, Fidel stated at the second FMC congress that the decision to create a women's organization in an underdeveloped country like ours had been a truly correct one, inasmuch as the tasks carried out by its members could not have been performed satisfactorily by other bodies.

With the launching of the federation, some people wondered if the existence of a specifically women's organization might not be discriminatory. However, experience has shown the decision to have been correct and necessary. The federation has served as one of the revolution's most important, best-suited vehicles for the integration into the revolutionary process of women, so cruelly exploited and discriminated against under capitalism. It was vital to wage an intensive and permanent effort to overcome ignorance, underestimation, and prejudice; and to enable women to discover themselves, to become aware of their own potential, to set forth and defend their views, to regard themselves as capable of undertaking difficult tasks, to lead, to create.

And although the gains made in the past fifteen years are considerable, it cannot be said that the goals have been fully attained. Women's participation in society must be in absolute equality with men, and so long as one vestige of inequality remains, it is necessary to continue to work to achieve this objective of the revolution.

II. Legal and Administrative Measures and Provisions Adopted by the Revolution in Favor of Women and Their Full Equality

With the victory of the revolution, the new revolutionary conditions and conceptions, together with the legal norms enacted in regard to women's rights, guaranteed them the right to work, to education, to health care, and to a rounded upbringing and education for their children. Specific guarantees for working women included equal pay for equal work, paid vacations, free access to all professions, social security, and other laws aimed at providing women with maximum protection as mothers and workers.

In order to provide for a just distribution of jobs between men and women, Ministry of Labor Resolutions 47 and 48 were enacted in 1968 to rationalize the work force so that all job positions would be adequately filled.

These resolutions guarantee a better integration of women; they keep women from those types of jobs whose characteristics might damage their biological function as mothers, or which could prove dangerous for the development of pregnancy and the growth of the baby. At present these resolutions are under study with a view to perfecting them.

Legislation guarantees men and women adequate protection through the established standards of safety and hygiene.

The maternity law guarantees women the effective enjoyment of maternity leave before and after they give birth—enough time for their own medical care and that of their newborn babies, and adequate income throughout this period.

With a view toward establishing as well women's full equality within the family—the basic cell of society—and to show the important role played by this institution in socialism, on March 8, 1975, the revolutionary government enacted the Family Code, which establishes the juridical norms that govern family relations in our proletarian state.

The Family Code enshrines the equality of women in marriage, eliminates the difference between legitimate and illegitimate children, and justly defines the rights and duties of the spouses as well as the equal obligations in regard to the children.

It also establishes that:

"Both partners must care for the family they have created and each must cooperate with the other in the education, upbringing, and guidance of the children according to the principles of socialist morality. They must participate, to the extent of their capacity or possibilities, in the running of the home, and cooperate so that it will develop in the best possible way."

In regard to political rights, women can vote and run for elected office, with no discriminatory rules that prevent them from holding any post in the leadership of the government, the party, or the political and mass organizations.

Likewise the law includes the right of women to take part in the defense of our homeland, to belong to the civilian defense units, to enroll voluntarily in the general military service, to take military studies, to belong to the reserve, and to join units of the FAR [Revolutionary Armed Forces] in wartime.

The revolution alone has made the equality of women before the law a reality—as enshrined in laws promulgated over the past years.

The draft constitution, which after the national referendum will become our fundamental law,* states in the chapter on equality:

"All citizens have equal rights and are subject to equal duties.

"Discrimination because of race, color, sex or national origin is forbidden and is punished by law. . . .

"Women have the same rights as men in the economic, political and social fields as well as in the family."

III. Objective and Subjective Elements that Impede the Full Participation of Women

Analysis of the Current Problems of Working Women

The socialist revolution has laid the foundations that guarantee the rights of women, placing them on a footing of full equality with men. But do women really exercise all these rights? What are the factors that prevent this from being so?

As was exhaustively examined at the Second Congress of the FMC, situations of inequality persist not only as a consequence of material difficulties, which will be eliminated in the process of economic development, but also because views and attitudes are frequently held that are out of keeping with the postulates and laws of our socialist society.

A fundamental battle must be waged in the field of consciousness, because backward ideas that we have dragged with us from the past continue to exist there.

Discrimination against women goes back many centuries—since, with the disintegration of the primitive community and the establishment of private property and the division of society into classes, men attained economic supremacy, and with it, social predominance.

Through the different regimes based on the exploitation of man by man, women were relegated to the narrow framework of the household. They were discriminated against and had limited possibilities for participating in social production, or were mercilessly exploited.

These ideas, which prevailed in our country until the overthrow

*The Cuban constitution was ratified February 15, 1976, in a national referendum of all citizens sixteen years and older. It was approved by 95.7 percent of the voters.

of the capitalist system, have no place in the stage of building the new society.

Both in their integration as a permanent labor force and in the countless voluntary tasks that have been carried out over the years, women have unquestionably demonstrated their sense of responsibility, their intellectual capacity, their potential for leadership, their determination, steadfastness, and dynamism.

Hundreds of thousands of compañeras have overcome real difficulties in order to become fully integrated into revolutionary tasks and to make their contribution to socialist construction.

They have participated in the creative work of education and culture.

They have shown that they are able to lead, to develop economic plans, to carry out party tasks.

They have shared the same battle trenches in the face of enemy aggression, ready to give their lives for the revolution.

Cuban women have fully demonstrated that they are able to successfully carry out whatever tasks are assigned to them.

Therefore, it is necessary for the party, state bodies, enterprises, and political and mass organizations to see to it that unjust criteria or decisions are not applied that run counter to the revolution's intention of ending women's inequality.

In this regard, the following currently existing situations which involve limitations on women's full incorporation into social activity, should be the object of attention so that just solutions can be reached in each case:

• When men are given preference over women in filling jobs, with the pretext that "women have lots of problems."

• When, in deciding who is to be promoted to a political or administrative responsibility, women are denied this right to avoid possible future difficulties arising from limitations connected with taking care of the home and the family.

• When an exemplary compañera is incorrectly judged for having joined the militia late or for having failed to take part in permanent work mobilizations, voluntary work, or formal study, without taking into account that she alone cared for young children, or sick or old family members.

• When valuable compañeras are unfairly criticized on the basis of false views regarding so-called moral problems.

Housework, an Unjust Overload of Work for Women

The first three cases are examples of an expression of inequality that establishes an unjust situation for women. We are talking about the overload of work assumed by the working woman when she alone performs all the housework after her workday, inasmuch as this involves a limitation on her participation and means a far greater energy outlay for her.

If we add to that the amount of time she spends traveling from home to work, taking the children to the day-care center or to school, doing the food and other shopping, washing, ironing, cooking, cleaning, taking care of the children, taking care of the sick and elderly persons in the family, it is clear that she will have to make a very great effort to study, and will have very little or no time to take part in cultural or recreational activities or to rest. Add to this, in many cases, the time required by her activities in the political and mass organizations.

It is a very different situation for women in those homes where the entire family shares in the housework on the basis of relations of full equality and comradeship—a fundamental factor in the success of marriage and in raising children in the just principles established by the revolution.

A survey of 251 working women taken in April of this year showed that they spend an average of thirteen hours a day from Monday through Friday on job-related and household activities, and eleven-and-a-half hours on weekends, due to the accumulation of housework.

Incorporation and Permanence of Women in the Work Force

Society needs the contribution of all its members, both men and women, in order to overcome underdevelopment.

The creation of the necessary material conditions that depend upon economic development, will be attained more rapidly to the extent that a larger number of women contribute to the productive process.

With a view to assessing the efforts made in building a work force of over 600,000 working women, the results of the incorporation and permanence of women in the work force in the 1969-74 period are shown as follows:

Year	Incorporation	Net increase	Decrease
1969	106,258	25,477	
1970	124,504	55,310	

Year	Incorporation	Net increase	Decrease
1971	86,188	—	63,174†
1972	130,843	37,263	
1973	138,437	72,279	
1974	127,694	69,748	
Total	713,924	196,903	

As the statistics indicate, along with the positive aspect of incorporation, there is a negative one: a large number of women, including trained professionals and technicians, leave productive activity, pressured by the objective and subjective difficulties they face in their family and social environment.

In order to attain a net increase of 196,903 women workers in the 1969-74 period, it was necessary for 713,924 women to join the work force.

No revolutionary should be indifferent to the fact that women leave their jobs, both because of the harm done to economic plans and to the development of the revolutionary consciousness of women and the people in general.

Rights and Duties of Working Women

The full enjoyment of their rights signifies the fulfillment of honorable duties for working women. Women need to understand this reality and realize that their difficulties will be eased in part to the extent that the state is able to allocate resources for the expansion of institutions and services that provide solutions to many of the working family's problems.

These resources will be the result of the increase in production and productivity, and this will be achieved precisely through the contribution of everyone.

Men and women, in this new society, have the duty to work conscientiously, uphold work discipline, fulfill the quota or task, boost productivity, upgrade the quality of production, take care of and strengthen socialist property, and take part enthusiastically

†This figure does not correspond exactly to 1971 since it includes data on women leaving the work force going back to 1967. In 1971 all the records of women who had left their jobs were updated, so that many administrators submitted to the National Bank of Cuba a list of those definitive departures from work that had not been reported previously. [Note in original.]

in emulation* in order to promote production and improve the quality of services.

Some Material Solutions for the Problems of Working Families

The revolution has worked hard to ease the burden of housework and guarantee better child care through creating institutions and providing services.

The day-care centers, semiboarding schools, boarding schools, workers' canteens, systems giving working women shopping priority through the CTC-MINCIN cards,** pre-made-up orders at food stores, and the special plans in laundries and cleaners have all contributed to this objective.

A total of 654 child-care centers operated in the country during the 1974-75 school year, benefitting nearly 55,000 children from 47,926 families.

Semiboarding schools have a total enrollment of 220,800 children, while the Ministry of Education boarding schools and the Camilo Cienfuegos military schools have an enrollment of 298,000, not counting similar facilities operated by other bodies.

At present the Pioneers have vacation plans, camps, and special areas for the children of working women.

Plans for the next five-year period include the construction of 400 day-care centers, which will bring total enrollment up to about 150,000; several hundred semiboarding schools; scores of homes for the elderly and special schools for the disabled.

By 1980, boarding schools will have capacity for about 700,000 students.

Given the country's material resources and all the other needs that must be met, it is not possible at the present time to do much more in this area. These figures signify large-scale efforts, and while we realize they do not meet our needs, they do represent the maximum possibilities for the 1976-80 period.

In addition to the increase in child-care facilities and schools, recent years have witnessed a better utilization of available services and the enlargement of the already existing ones.

---

*Emulation is a term for the many types of collective competition in Cuba; its goal is to benefit society as a whole rather than individuals. There are emulations in the fields of production, education, health care, etc.

**A union membership card issued by the Central Organization of Cuban Trade Unions and the Ministry of Domestic Commerce. This plan gives working women preference in shopping.

Sales of refrigerators, stoves, washers, food processors, sewing machines, and other appliances have also increased.

These solutions, which have required large-scale efforts and resources from the state, are still insufficient to cover the needs arising from the incorporation of women into the work force. *Therefore, we are considering recommending to the proper bodies that they study the following proposals, for possible application in the next few years:*

• Increasing the vacation and weekend plans for children, increasing the hours of the semiboarding schools, and other solutions designed to upgrade the care of children, the sick, and the elderly.

• Increasing certain kinds of industrial and food services that could ease housework.

• Studying the suitability of establishing throughout the country special hours in services, stores, laundromats, cleaners, appliance repairs, etc., for working women.

• Studying the opening and closing times of stores in order to apply all over the country the hours most suited to the needs of working women.

• Reviewing the functioning of the pre-made-up grocery order (shopping bag plan) and the CTC-MINCIN card in order to introduce changes arising from experience and the current situation of supplies.

• Increasing and improving quality in the service provided by dry cleaners and laundries, including the self-service laundromats.

• Increasing the supply of articles that facilitate housework for working families.

• Studying the possibility of importing or producing nationally fabrics with a blend of synthetic fibers in order to ease the work of washing, drying, and ironing, especially when it comes to children's uniforms.

• Targeting sales of industrial goods for the home and some for personal use that are in very short supply, in order to benefit working women whose work schedules make it hard for them to acquire these any other way.

• Studying the possibility of creating a service of home plumbing repairs, electricity, carpentry, masonry, upholstery, etc., which would alleviate household burdens.

• Analyzing the introduction of evening hours for gynecological and obstetrical appointments. Include pediatric appointments in this study.

• Increasing, in workplaces with the proper conditions, children's areas for organizing vacation plans and day camps for the children of working women on Saturdays, and during the school holidays and vacations.

• Increasing and improving the quality of the day camps held at semiboarding schools.

• Providing greater information on the benefits provided and the hours of the special services set up for working women.

Care and Education of the Children: The Responsibility of Both Parents

Notwithstanding the big investments made in these plans, they still fail to meet the mounting needs of a population eager to take part in and contribute to the revolution.

In addition, it is absolutely vital for men and women to share the responsibility for the care for and education of the children. It is a pedagogical and psychological fact that girls and boys need their mothers and their fathers equally.

The view that child rearing is the exclusive responsibility of mothers must be rejected. The beautiful responsibility of caring for them, watching over their school work, attending parents' meetings, getting to know their friends, their way of thinking, guiding them in life, bringing them up in revolutionary principles, is a duty contracted equally by both father and mother.

When both parents have responsibilities in social production, the proper bodies must foster the conditions for working men and women to share in the care of sick children both at home and in the hospital.

Attitude Regarding the Need for Women's Incorporation

All the solutions that can help to ease the burden of housework will facilitate greater participation by women and men in economic, social, political, and cultural activities. *But the current material limitations must not be an excuse for failure to tackle various problems that could be solved—at least in part—and which depend on the attitudes toward the incorporation and permanence of women in production held by those who are representing the revolutionary power at all levels of the state and political apparatus throughout the country.*

Unfortunately, in practice, not everyone displays such an awareness. In order to develop it, a consistent ideological effort must be maintained, which, logically, should be led by the members of the party and the Young Communists in close coordination with the state bodies and the mass organizations.

Socialist Emulation; The Working Mother

There are some matters that should receive special attention; for example, the encouragement of the double function fulfilled by working women, especially mothers, who—at the same time that they care for their children—also fulfill their duty to contribute to society by doing their best to perform their jobs efficiently. These women unquestionably deserve special recognition from all our people.

In addition, they often perform all the housework, because, as we have reiterated in this document, in many homes these tasks are still not shared. However, there are frequent concrete expressions that show a lack of understanding of the problems of these women in their workplaces. This happens when similar demands are mechanically made for working women with children as for the rest of the workers when it comes to analyzing justified absences, voluntary work, or study, applying the same standards to both categories of workers. In setting standards for socialist emulation, it is necessary to eliminate schematic criteria which do not take into account the real difficulties that working women confront and which therefore deprive them of the incentives to which they are entitled.

It is necessary to analyze the participation of women, especially working mothers, in socialist emulation, taking their difficulties into account so that these do not mean downgrading the women or their workplaces.

Analysis of the Job Situation; Training and Upgrading

At present, one of the circumstances that seriously hinders the incorporation of women into the work force is the lack of training of thousands of women willing to work.

A premise for overcoming this situation is the technical and educational training of unemployed women so they can be on an equal footing and take skilled jobs.

Furthermore, it is vital to study the possibility of upgrading women's skills on the job, so they can be able to take on positions of greater responsibility.

In studying the employment structure, we find that of every 100 workers, only 25.3 are women.

The structure of employment shows the following:

Table 1
Percentage of each sex by occupation

Job Category	Total	Women	Men
Manual workers	100%	11.6%	88.4%
Service workers	100	48.7	51.3
Technicians	100	49.1	50.9
Administrative	100	67.5	32.5
Managers	100	15.3	84.7

Table 2

Body	Total	Men	Women	% of women
Light Industry	88,133	49,073	39,060	44.3%
Cubatabaco	49,310	22,473	26,837	54.4
INIT [Natl. Inst. of Tourism]	79,177	46,823	32,354	40.9
MINSAP [Min. of Public Health]	131,005	47,577	83,428	63.6
MINED [Min. of Education]	224,694	91,864	132,830	59.1

Table 3
Distribution of working women
in job categories by percentage

Body	Total	Manual	Service	Tech.	Admin.	Mgr.
Light Industry	100%	81%	2%	4%	10%	3%
Cubatabaco	100	93	1	1	4	1
INIT	100	23	65	2	6	4
MINSAP	100	8	41	42	6	3
MINED	100	4	22	65	5	4

In comparing Tables 1 and 3 we could conclude that the participation of women is linked to their qualifications, since the INIT, which requires no skills, has 65 percent women in services and 23 percent as manual workers. Table 1 shows low percentages of women in those sectors that require training.

It must be stressed that there are high levels of job skills in MINSAP and MINED and that the largest number of women workers are to be found in these agencies.

What really is evident is the low level of women in leadership posts in all bodies, including those with a high percentage of women workers, thus underscoring the fact that we still have to attain the goals set forth by the revolution of having women take their rightful place in keeping with their level and development.

Some Organizational Measures and Possible Forms of Employment Designed to Make It Easier for Women Workers to Meet Their Obligations

We recommend to all the proper bodies the study and possible application of the following measures:

• Organization of special courses for the upgrading of working women during hours that enable those who face some difficulties to participate.

• Inclusion of the need for women workers when drawing up the programs of the work-force agencies, with strict control checks of compliance with these programs, as well as the implantation of courses for the incorporation of unemployed women in installed capacities and in projected new facilities.

• Establishment of part-time hours that will enable women to take jobs of less than eight hours. A study should be made to see if part-time hours could also be applied to women who must leave their jobs after their maternity leave is up because of a lack of vacancies in the day-care centers.

• Establishment of new forms of work: by contract, piecework, or even at home, according to the requirements and possibilities of the economy.

• Implementation of free Saturdays as long as the production and services involved permit it,* and the proper conditions exist at the workplaces. This would be warranted inasmuch as on the basis of current experience, the presence of children at workplaces represents a risk to the children, hinders the work of their mothers and their mothers' co-workers, and is therefore detrimental to production and services.

• Bringing the number of workers employed into line with the real needs of the workplaces with a majority of women, and changing this figure where necessary since thus far, in many cases, the existing number of workers still fails to cover the needs arising from maternity leaves, vacation, sickness of women workers or members of their families, etc. This personnel shortfall places an extra burden on the other women workers.

*Cuban workers generally work a 5½-day workweek—eight hours a day during the week and half a day on Saturday.

IV. Difficulties in the Promotion of Women to Administrative and Political Leadership Posts

People's Power; Participation of Women

On July 26, 1974, in his speech on the twenty-first anniversary of the glorious attack on the Moncada Barracks, Fidel analyzed the low percentage of women elected to the People's Power assemblies in Matanzas, pointing out:

". . . It shows how women still suffer from certain discrimination and inequality, how we still have residues of cultural backwardness and how we still retain old thinking patterns in the back of our minds."

If we analyze the experience achieved by a large number of women in the work of the mass organizations, their familiarity with community problems, their broad possibilities for developing useful work in these bodies, we reach the conclusion that an effort needs to be made to keep the Matanzas situation from being repeated.

Last April research began on the reasons why more women were not elected to the municipal assemblies. Some 635 interviews were conducted with 302 men and 333 women chosen from the voter registration lists in the municipalities of Matanzas Province.

The most interesting results included the following: When asked to state what factors hindered women from holding leadership posts, one of the most common replies of the voters was:

"They are responsible for housework and caring for their children and their husbands" (59.6 percent).

Also worthy of mention is the high percentage of people who mentioned the lack of publicity on the possibility of electing women and evaluating their qualifications (32 percent).

It is also significant that the characteristic *"having their housework and child care tasks solved or facilitated"* was mentioned in the case of women by 20 percent of the persons polled, while no mention of this was made in the case of men.

When women voters were asked if they would have been prepared to take on that responsibility had they been elected, 45.7 percent replied affirmatively while 54.3 percent said no. If the figure of women who were willing is compared with the 7.6 percent of the actual nominees who were women, it will be seen that real possibilities existed for greater participation.

The majority of the women who said no did so on the basis of *"housework and care for the children and husband"* as the main obstacle. This reply, along with the factor of low educational level, accounts for the highest percentage of replies.

In the question pertaining to the reasons for the failure to nominate more women to run for delegate, once again the main weight went to the *"responsibility traditionally reserved to the female sex"* when it comes to household tasks and caring for the children (33.8 percent).

In regard to the necessary characteristics for holding leadership positions, if we compare those mentioned for men and for women, it will be seen that among both, the requirement of being "moral, serious-minded, decent" was mentioned by 45 percent as a requirement for women while only 20 percent of those polled mentioned it in the case of men.

In some cases women limited themselves by turning down a responsibility assigned to them, at times due to a lack of development, but in the majority of cases, because of domestic problems.

There is no question that the replies we are analyzing are to a large extent based on traditionalist, prejudice-ridden ideas that involve considerations that we will deal with in greater depth further on in this thesis.

Analysis of the percentages of women leaders in the party, the UJC, and the mass organizations

Levels	PCC	UJC	CTC	CDR	ANAP
Municipal	2.9%	22%	24%	7%	16.38%
Regional	4.1	7	21	7	0.76
Provincial	6.3	7	15	3	1.19
National	5.5	10	7	19	2.04

The statistics on the percentage of women leaders of the Young Communist League are eloquent, even though they are not in line with the 29 percent female membership.

In the party, 13.23 percent of the members are women, while the percentage of women leaders is still lower.

Also significant is the low percentage of women leaders of the CDRs, 50 percent of whose members are women.

In the unions, the percentages are encouraging.

The [women's] federation itself confronts problems regarding the promotion and stability of cadres, and this has a bigger impact on its work in view of the fact that all of its leaders are women.

On many occasions, when a compañera is promoted to higher levels, it proves difficult to select the woman with the greatest merit and capacity for the job. This is often the case because of the natural difficulties that arise when a cadre is promoted, especially when a change of residence is involved; and in the case of the married woman, they are really insoluble—in many cases due to a lack of understanding of the value of her work, be it on the part of husband or family, the management at the husband's workplace, the agency that must facilitate the change in housing, etc.

The data on the limited participation of women at the different leadership levels of the political and mass organizations shows the need to carry out a profound ideological effort with a view to changing this situation.

Promotion in the State Bodies

As for the state bodies, the tendency is the same as in the case of the political and mass organizations.

The most commonly expressed opinion in the case of the state bodies regarding the reasons why women do not hold leadership responsibilities is: "there has been no systematic effort on the part of these bodies to promote and encourage the incorporation of women into leadership posts"; "in addition, there are limitations of a social nature determined by housework; taking care of the children; the lack of sufficient day-care facilities, semiboarding schools, boarding schools, etc., as well as other services such as laundries, etc."

In order to obtain a more exact idea of the factors involved in the limited participation of women in leadership, a survey was taken through the CTC at 211 workplaces throughout the country of 5,168 men and women workers from all sectors of the economy.

The replies that appeared with greatest frequency were as follows:

• 83 percent regarded caring for the children as the limiting factor.

• *85.7 percent mentioned housework as the limiting factor.*

• 59 percent said that increased responsibility meant staying at work for longer periods of time.

• 51.1 percent felt it is due to the fact that women have a low educational level.

• 22.8 percent indicated that the administration takes the view that the limitations of housework and caring for the children keep women from holding such posts since this would have an adverse effect on their work.

• 38 percent felt that there is no policy of promoting women to leadership posts.

• 26.2 percent felt that accepting responsibility would lead to problems with the women's husbands.

The result of the survey, together with the general situation posed by the promotion of women in state bodies, reflects the presence of material problems that hinder promotion, as well as a lack of understanding of the need for women to hold leadership posts.

Because of the above, we recommend:

1. The mapping out of a promotion policy, since at present over 600,000 women are overcoming the difficulties they face and are working in different sectors of the economy and services.

2. The improvement and expansion of some services.

3. The development of a profound ideological effort geared to having housework shared by all family members.

Educational Level of Women

In analyzing this problem it should not be forgotten that in many cases the promotion of capable compañeras is hindered by their lack of the required educational and technical level.

Over the years since the victory of the revolution, big efforts have been made to upgrade the educational level of the female population, with the results so far as follows:

1970 census	*Men*	*Women*
Third grade or under	33.8%	37.4%
Fourth to sixth grade	46.7	43.7
Junior high school†	14.7	13.9
Technical and professional	2.5	1.6
Senior high school††	0.4	2.0
Higher education	1.7	1.2

It will be noted that in 1970, 81.1 percent of the female population had an educational level below that of the sixth grade, while just 13.9 percent had completed junior high school and only 4.8 percent had completed high school or gone beyond it.

In the CTC's census on the schooling of workers taken in 1974, we find the following data:

†Secondary school. [Note in original.]

††Technological, FOC, or regular senior high. [Note in original.]

Educational level attained by working women

Level	Men	Women
Under sixth grade	44.7%	27.0%
Sixth grade	25.7	24.0
Junior high incomplete	8.8	11.0
Junior high completed	7.2	11.0
FOC* incomplete	3.0	4.0
FOC completed	1.5	2.0
Senior high incomplete	2.7	7.0
Senior high completed	2.3	8.0
University incomplete	1.2	1.0
University completed	1.4	2.0
Language incomplete	1.1	2.0
Language completed	0.4	1.0

It will be noted that working women have attained considerable levels of schooling in comparison with their previous situation, although they are far from reaching the levels required for carrying forward the new tasks posed by our revolution.

Significantly, at present the average educational level of working women is higher than that of male workers. *These data from the 1970 census and the CTC's survey in regard to working women enable us to make comparative analyses and conclude that not only problems arising from a low level of schooling are involved. Access by women to more skilled and leadership positions is limited as well by prejudice and discrimination that still exist.*

Nevertheless, we should stress educational and technical advancement as a key factor for tackling the revolution's big tasks in the economic sphere.

Policy of Promoting Women
In keeping with our analysis on the promotion of women, and taking into account the data obtained from surveys and other statistics, it is clear that there needs to be a determined policy to promote women. To that end, we recommend·

1. That the state bodies, in coordination with the unions and the CTC, conduct a full study of the jobs that can be held by women and that they map out a plan for training and upgrading

*The Facultad Obrera-Campesina (Worker-Peasant Faculty) is a program of night classes for adults at the high school level.

in order to facilitate their promotion or their possibilities for placement.

This should encompass both immediate and long-range (five-year) plans for training and upgrading.

• Likewise, the percentages of women to be trained will be determined—in accordance with the worker-training programs, both immediate and long term (five-year plan)—keeping in mind the goal of changing the composition of the work force by providing women with greater possibilities.

• This study of the presence of women will be made, first of all, in the different spheres of production and services; and secondly, taking into account the increase of women in the work force that is forecast for the five-year period.

• In keeping with plans, the conditions should be created that will allow for the development of a program geared to the following:

—Training and upgrading of women, taking into account different levels, work schedules, and types of courses, including extension programs.

—The program for training women should be regarded as an important indicator in the overall plan of the different bodies, so that it can be checked as one aspect of each center's administrative efficiency.

—The sectors, agencies, and enterprises, together with the unions, CTC, and MINED, will promote educational upgrading (an indispensable precondition for the development of the training plans) with a minimum goal being the attainment by all workers of a sixth-grade level during the five-year period.

2. In the case of the political and mass organizations, it is also necessary to encourage the educational and political upgrading of women cadres.

3. In regard to the presence of women in leadership posts in the administrative, political, and mass organizations, it is necessary to recommend the following:

• *Mapping out an adequate promotion policy from the grass roots to the higher levels, with concrete goals geared to the current and future presence of women.*

• *Development of a broad political and ideological effort among men and women designed to promote greater awareness of the importance of women's full participation in leadership tasks, especially among women themselves.*

• *Promote a deeper awareness of the social and political importance of the goal expressed by the first secretary of our*

party, of increasing the participation of women in the different
levels of leadership in the People's Power assemblies that are to
be created all over the country.

V. Young Women; Young Women Professionals or Middle-Level Technicians Who Do Not Work; Idle Young Women

Young Women: Opportunities and Difficulties

We have analyzed different aspects of the difficulties women often face when it comes to fulfilling their duties and exercising their rights in full equality with men. And if these difficulties in general involve a heavy burden that hinders their participation, in the case of young women they are even worse, given these two key factors:

• that limitations linked with the care of young children are more prevalent in the case of young women;

• that these are young women educated by the revolution, which has invested considerable resources in educating them.

Our youth are educated from the first years of their schooling in the ideas of socialism, of sharing rights and duties in all different situations of life. There should be no lack of understanding on the part of the new generation, which benefits fully from all that the revolution offers, and which is being educated in the just principles of equality.

The revolution offers the possibility for study and work, but we must make efforts so that after a young woman becomes a mother she can continue to fulfill her duties to the revolution, returning to the people through her labor all that has been invested in her training.

The Young Professional Woman

When a young woman graduate has to leave her job or is unable to take a job, the loss is unquestionably much greater. It is painful for these young women to be frustrated, to be kept from living up to the hopes placed in them by the working people, to find that they are unable to develop fully and make their contribution to the development of the revolution's plans.

The party, the UJC, and the mass organizations should make a
special study of the circumstances that lead these young women
professionals or technicians to drop out of the work force, in order
to map out the measures to overcome these problems and to make

possible the reintegration of these young women in jobs of their training or specialization.

In addition, it is necessary for the bodies that train or place these working women to be aware of their family situations, especially motherhood, so that they can be employed more efficiently, and so that those factors that delay their working life or force them to leave it can be prevented.

As social solutions to household and family tasks are increased, the problems of young women professionals and technicians should receive special attention, although it should be stressed that many of these problems could begin to be solved through greater cooperation of the family in household tasks.

The party, the UJC, and the mass organizations should promote ideological work to make possible a more consistent attitude toward the solution of these problems, both on the part of revolutionaries who are around the young woman, and on her own part. This will help her to exercise her own rights and at the same time to fulfill her duty to her socialist homeland.

The Idle Young Woman

In contrast to the great majority of young women who develop at work and/or study and who play an active part in building the future, there still remain a number of idle young women. Despite the opportunity to study or work, they receive without giving anything in return, and they spend their youth without furthering their education, wasting the opportunities provided them to keep from falling behind.

We must work with these young women and their families in order to:

Promote their participation in the mass organizations and in community activities and try to incorporate them into upgrading and training courses whenever this is possible, with a view toward their incorporation into the work force.

Early Motherhood

In other cases young women leave the work force because of real difficulties, among which we can cite those arising from having children at a very early age.

Sometimes young women without adequate preparation prematurely confront a stage of life that requires all the maturity and responsibility of the couple. Young people that have hardly experienced life, some even less than sixteen years of age, sometimes pressured by false moral conceptions that still exist—whether through social or family environment or even their own prejudices—are wont to formalize through marriage a relationship that has not been established on a firm foundation.

In the majority of cases, these young women feel forced to abandon their studies for the responsibilities of motherhood, becoming constricted to the confines of the home.

It is necessary that young people of both sexes grow up with an adequate knowledge of the responsibility and the necessary precautions that go with a sexual relationship—both because of what early motherhood can mean for the educational, biological, psychological, and social development of the young woman; and because of the obligations stemming from the creation of a new human being—to which the couple that created it have unavoidable duties not always compatible with those that flow from their dedication to the tasks of their own educational and professional development.

Lack of Understanding Shown by Some Young People

Before the celebration of the Second Congress of the FMC, two surveys were carried out—one of 135 male university students and professionals and 507 female university students and technicians, all incorporated into the work force; and the other with 1,926 women not involved in any useful social task—with the aim of getting a deeper understanding of the causes of the difficulties that confront young women relating to their participation and advancement in society. Several comparisons were made: men and women, working women and women not working, technical/professional workers and nontechnical/nonprofessional workers.

Taking into account that all those interviewed were young people between the ages of 17 and 35, inclusively, it became evident that the majority of them understood the idea of women's equality, but in dealing with this same theme in questions reflecting daily life, it was observed that prejudices and discriminatory traditions still exist.

These contradictions that were observed show that, although understanding of the problem has advanced, it is still necessary to break with old ideas and reaffirm the necessity of undertaking in all fields a systematic educational effort on the principles of equality between men and women.

The youth, as Che said, constitute "the basic clay of our work," and from this flows the task of ideologically educating them in the high values of socialist morality.

For this reason, it is important for every revolutionary to set an example through their militant attitude and their readiness to rid themselves of old ideas and embrace the just principles of the new morality.

The Need for the Family to Share Housework

Throughout this document we have seen time and time again that the factor that limits a woman's access to leadership responsibilities, to her development in an office or a profession, is the fact that in many homes the housework and the care of the children fall on her shoulders *alone.*

This unjust situation becomes graver still when it also prevents her from attending training, retraining, or upgrading courses necessary to take on many jobs or to be promoted.

In other words, the overload of work, in itself a situation of inequality, at the same time is often a major factor in each one of the other problems of inequality we have analyzed.

In his article "A Great Beginning," published in Moscow in July 1919, Lenin described housework and its effect on the woman: "Notwithstanding all the laws emancipating woman, she continues to be a *domestic slave,* because *petty housework* crushes, strangles, stultifies and degrades her, chains her to the kitchen and the nursery, and she wastes her labour on barbarously unproductive, petty, nerve-racking, stultifying and crushing drudgery."

• *Making an equitable distribution of the inevitable household tasks is an unavoidable revolutionary obligation of the present time.* Some of the domestic tasks will be taken over by state services and institutions in keeping with our country's economic and social development.

Currently, these tasks take long hours and it is a deep injustice that in many homes still, these tedious and burdensome though necessary and indispensable tasks are all done by the woman, when a collective effort by members of the family would reduce the heavy burden that falls on her—a double burden in the case of the working woman—and in both cases a limitation on her ability to fulfill her duties to our society.

It is necessary for everyone to understand that this is not something that concerns only the future generation; it applies to all members of our society today, for these collective solutions based on comradeship, consideration, and mutual respect are in and of themselves part of the upbringing of the current and future generations. At the same time, they will also open up for women opportunities for access to education, culture, social life, and—in the case of housewives—useful social work.

Important advances of our revolution have been achieved in

creating material solutions to the problems of the family and in raising the ideological level of our people. *But it is necessary that those that still have not understood the just principles of equality on which our socialist society is based, get rid of their prejudices and atavistic ideas and understand that men and women are equal in conditions and possibilities; that both have equal capacities to lead and to build; that masculinity is not in contradiction with housework, taking care of children, and mutual cooperation in all fields of revolutionary activity, but rather is reaffirmed through them; that femininity is not counterposed to any activity of work, of educational improvement, or of the responsibilities of daily life.*

This effort is part of basic human relations and is an intimate aspect of socialist morality, whose principles today have begun to be a guide for the life and the conduct of men and women.

VI. Socialist Morality and Women's Equality

A New Morality

Discrimination because of sex is characteristic of the hypocritical bourgeois morality of exploiting societies.

The victory of the socialist revolution necessarily implies the triumph of a new morality in line with the economic, political, and social changes corresponding to the interests and ideas of the proletariat. For this reason, a consistent struggle against those things that are antiquated and unjust must be waged throughout all of society.

Our people have been able to destroy capitalism and make the revolution, to do away with the exploitation of man by man once and for all, and they must also be able to achieve victory in the field of ideas, attaining the full equality of women.

Socialist morality, determined by the people's interest, is compatible only with that which helps destroy exploitation, injustice, misery, lack of education, and that helps establish new relations of fraternity among human beings, which consolidates the new society: socialism.

The abolition of private property in the means of production, the elimination of all the ties of dependency to imperialism, and the creation of new relations of production, provide a solid basis for affirming and developing new moral conceptions.

Exploitation, parasitism, living without working, consuming without producing, living off the sweat and sacrifice of others— are immoral.

Socialist morality is not compatible with individualism, abuse, egoistic ambitions, dishonesty, lack of care of social property, immodesty, or compromising with the enemies of socialism and the homeland.

Neither is it moral to foster discrimination, inequality, and injustice; and since the existence of an overload of work for the woman and the comfort of the other family members at her expense constitutes an injustice, we also affirm that this is in contradiction to socialist morality, as is placing obstacles to the participation of women in all spheres of social life.

The standards of socialist morality are the same for every citizen. However, in many cases still, flowing from the conceptions of bourgeois morality, men and women are judged differently for the same deed.

It is unjust to apply different criteria to men and women relating to so-called moral problems that have to do with sexual relations.

It is necessary for all to understand that what is to be censurable for her is also censurable for him. There cannot exist one morality for women and another one for men; this is contrary to Marxist-Leninist ideology, to the principles of this revolution.

It is not correct to judge the woman differently from the man; what is socially acceptable for the man must be equally acceptable for the woman.

The epoch is gone of economic dependency, of mercantile relations, of being tied together for special interests, of marriages maintained by prejudice or formalism, when neither love nor respect exist.

Men and women have to be equally free and responsible in determining their relations in the area of their sexual lives.

This freedom does not imply licentiousness, which degrades beauty and the relations between men and women. Relations within the couple under socialism flow from a different idea: they are established on the basis of equality, sincerity, and mutual respect, and have to be based on clear and advanced ideas about the responsibility involved in sexual relations—the origin of life and the creator of the new generations.

VII. Ideological Work to Be Done

Necessary Transformation of Mass Consciousness

In analyzing the question of women's equality, we can see that the difficulties are caused by an interrelationship of different factors that are analyzed in this thesis: the objective factors, of extreme importance, which the socialist state is striving strongly to gradually solve; and the subjective factors, those that bear down on the consciousness of men and women—these are decisive to a large degree since they determine the attitude toward the problems and how to confront and resolve them.

The fact that the necessary and proper changes in the people's consciousness have not been accomplished constitutes an obstacle to the realization of equality between men and women made possible by the revolution.

On many occasions, programs, songs, and different types of events are still presented by the mass media in which the image of women we inherited from capitalism is portrayed: a sexual and decorative object, passive, confined to the tasks of the home, whose highest aspiration is marriage.

Many statements have been made over the years, which are reaffirmed in this thesis, about the need to eliminate the exhibition of women, which besides being negative and absurd in our society, sometimes becomes vulgar and grotesque.

An example of this is the beauty contests and the wrong types of exhibitions that are carried out during the carnivals.

It is necessary that these forms be eliminated and substituted by others in keeping with today's conception of women.

If we begin from the standpoint of Marx and Martí that labor shapes the human being, we must be concerned that there are still women in our country who do work that does not contribute either to their own development or to the rest of society. We must make the necessary efforts to guarantee that all recreational performances, without losing the tone that corresponds to them as recreational, be artistic events, for there are still some productions whose form and content do not differ in any way from the spectacles of the capitalist mold that were introduced in our country during the pseudorepublic and that should not exist now, inasmuch as they correspond to a decadent society.

Taking this into account, we recommend that the transformation of these events be studied, especially the carnivals, since these are a recreational activity in which all the people participate.

Educational Work

To eliminate once and for all the prejudices and discrimination against women which are a heritage of capitalism and the other exploitative social regimes that preceded it, and to guarantee that the new generations grow up free of prejudices, brought up in the just principles of socialism, all possible measures must be undertaken to carry out a profound, systematic, and permanent ideological effort designed to educate the masses, to educate the family.

The party, the UJC, and the mass organizations will have to systematically develop an ideological program designed to educate children, youth, and adults in the highest principles of equality and fraternity that should exist among men and women, supporting this work with the consistent utilization of the mass media.

During the discussions of the thesis of the Second Congress of the Federation of Cuban Women, one of the questions debated with greatest interest was that relating to the family under socialism. In every instance, both in these debates and in the changes and additions proposed, the limitations of the parents and teachers were sharply revealed when it came to answering or elaborating on many themes of an elementary pedagogical and psychological content that are indispensable for a proper education of children and youth, those relating, above all, to sexual themes.

In order to respond to these problems, a plan must be developed that should include all the aspects necessary for a rounded education for all ages, preparing teachers and parents so that they can conduct educational work along these lines, as well as higher level support personnel and counselors. To also prepare the necessary publications and a program of illustrated texts along these lines, making an adequate use of the mass media.

It is necessary that we continually improve the education of our young generation in the highest principles and values of the society that we are creating: loyalty to the socialist homeland, love of our history and the traditions of struggle of our people, the constant practice of proletarian internationalism, and the consistent and firm defense of the ideology of the proletariat.

Young Cubans must ground themselves in the profound ideological concepts of Marxism-Leninism about the equality of women and the appreciation of the role of the human couple in all its dignity and beauty.

Part of this education, which has to be imparted in the home and school, must be an adequate sexual education at each stage of the child's life, so that marriage and the family are established on solid foundations.

The concept of women's equality in all fields begins to be

created in the home with the attitude of the couple, their mutual relations, and the education that they offer their children.

Fidel has said that women merit special consideration from society, that their condition as mother and the natural sacrifices this entails in and of itself must not be forgotten, that "there must exist proletarian chivalry, proletarian courtesy, proletarian manners, and proletarian consideration of women."

The habits of special respect that women merit, must be maintained at all times by each one of the members of this country of workers, and have to be inculcated in the child from the earliest age.

These are the fundamental aspects of the efforts to be carried out as part of the plan we are referring to.

This plan will have to contain a systematic educational program with the children, starting from the day-care center and the first grades in school, so that from early on they share in the household tasks, and learn the rights and responsibilities that they have within the family, giving them a real picture of the origin of life and its different stages of development, instilling in them mutual respect between the sexes, which will permit them to arrive at a stable and happy marriage based on deepgoing love and honesty, as well as loyalty to the just principles of a socialist society, where motherhood and fatherhood, correctly conceived, are the basis of the family, the essential nucleus of society.

The Struggle for Equality: A Task for Everyone

It is necessary for all the political and mass bodies and organizations that are involved in bringing up and educating the individual, especially children and youth, to undertake the joint educational plan that, embracing all the aspects related to achieving a rounded education, answers the need to eliminate the holdovers of the ideology of our class enemy.

As Fidel said on closing the Second Congress of the FMC:

"We all believe that this struggle against discrimination of women, this struggle for women's equality and for women's integration, must be carried out by the whole society. And it is the task of our party, in the first place; it is the task of our educational institutions and it is the task of all our mass organizations."

And later he affirmed:

". . . in order to achieve those objectives, women and men must struggle together, women and men have to become seriously and profoundly aware of the problem. They have to wage that

battle together. And we are certain that it will be waged and that it will be won!"

The communist militants in their high responsibility, must carry the banner of this ideological battle, through their political work directed to the collective that surrounds them or that they lead, and, above all, through their example.

Above, day-care center; below, Pioneers

Into the Third Decade

Fidel Castro

At its founding in 1960, the Federation of Cuban Women numbered 17,000 members. By the time of its Third Congress, held March 5-8, 1980, its membership approached two-and-a-half million, 80 percent of all Cuban women over the age of fourteen.

The period between the FMC's second and third congresses was one of advancement for the Cuban revolution. On the domestic front, the economy continued to progress and the Cuban people saw an increase in their standard of living. There were big developments internationally as well. In 1979, popular revolutions took place in Nicaragua and Grenada. After twenty years of persistent work in conditions of isolation within the hemisphere, Cubans felt that they were no longer alone, and this knowledge gave them added inspiration to pursue their revolutionary goals.

In his speech closing the congress, Castro examined women's gains in winning genuine equality, while at the same time pointing to the objective and subjective obstacles that still existed in this regard. In discussing the advances made in incorporating women into the work force, he mentioned as a limiting factor the problem of finding jobs for everyone that needed them. This employment problem is completely different from what working people face in the United States. In Cuba, permanent structural unemployment does not exist: there are no business cycles, recessions, or plant closings caused by employers seeking to make a higher profit somewhere else. Eliminating that type of unemployment has been one of the main gains of the Cuban revolution. In fact, for most of the more than twenty years since the revolution, Cuba has faced a labor shortage. However, as a result of the postrevolution "baby boom" generation coming of work age in the late 1970s, Cuba faced a conjunctural problem of providing jobs for all these youth. In his speech, Castro outlined the revolution's approach to solving this problem.

In looking to the future, Castro noted Cuba's plans for continued progress as well as the difficulties the country faced related both to the series of blights affecting Cuban agriculture and livestock and to the growing international polarization between imperialism and the forces for revolutionary change throughout the world.

The following excerpts from Castro's March 8, 1980, closing speech are reprinted from Granma Weekly Review, *March 16, 1980.*

Distinguished guests;
Comrades of the party and government leadership;
Dear comrades:
First of all, I want to express our deepest appreciation to the many delegations from all the continents that have honored and accompanied us at this congress. I also want to warmly congratulate them and you on this International Women's Day. [*Applause*] I think there couldn't have been a better way to celebrate this date than with the conclusion of this great congress. The congress has been a brilliant review of everything Cuban women have signified, signify now, and will signify in the revolution.

It wouldn't be possible to write the history of our revolution in the last twenty years without mentioning the Federation of Cuban Women. There is virtually no activity in which it has not participated in one way or the other; no activity, even those which are viewed as the almost exclusive domain of men: war and national defense, for example. Here, as in Nicaragua, Namibia, El Salvador, or Grenada, women are playing an active role. It is enough to mention some of those tasks, many of which were mentioned here and which are very important. For example, raising women's educational level, going from the literacy drive in 1961, in which Cuban women played such an outstanding role, and the first schools for peasant women which were organized by the federation and from which hundreds of thousands of women graduated. The change in peasant women was evident—in their spirit, in their way of thinking and way of life, even in the most remote regions of the country. Even the way they dressed changed with the clothes they learned to make in the schools, a program that has continued over twenty years now. Then there are the struggle, the efforts, and the gains in the battle for the sixth grade and beyond, for intermediate and university studies. In this connection it is interesting to note that 31 percent of working women are studying, while only 25 percent of men are. [*Applause*]

It isn't that men have things to do which make it more difficult for them to study. The difference is present in workplaces with normal shifts. So we have more women studying than men.

What's more, through these programs, hundreds of thousands of women have acquired skills which make it possible for them to do useful things, useful for themselves and useful for the country; things that are economically promising as shown, for example, by the growing number of handicrafts produced in the People's Power workshops.

Together with the effort to improve women's cultural and technical knowledge, there has been a drive to further their ideological development. How would it have been possible to bring about Cuban women's present level of political and revolutionary awareness without the work of the FMC? How could we have carried revolutionary ideas, the principles of Marxism-Leninism, en masse, to the working women and housewives without the constant and tenacious effort of the FMC? How could we have trained so many thousands of cadres who supervise the work of the organization at different levels? How could so many women have distinguished themselves in our society? How could so many cadres have been trained, not only for the work of the organization itself, but to contribute on the different fronts of the revolution? This work is also seen among the leadership cadres in general thanks to the work done by the federation's schools, including the national school of the federation, a school in which, by the way, two-thirds of the student body comes from other countries, [*Applause*] chiefly from Africa, although all continents are represented. [*Applause*]

We have worked hard, and only by working tirelessly has it been possible to raise the political and revolutionary awareness of Cuban women to its present level.

I repeat, this wouldn't have been possible without the federation's work.

The federation's activity is also felt on other fronts, such as one frequently mentioned here: crime prevention and eradication, work with children, and the efforts of the 12,754 women social workers, cadres who were trained to work in this important field. Lately the party leadership has also been considering this issue: what sort of institutions we should set up in addition to the reeducation centers; what sort of cases should be handled by the Ministry of Education, in ordinary schools; which ones should be handled by the Ministry of Education in schools set up for this purpose; what experiences the other socialist countries have on this score. This is a very important issue and a great responsibility for the party and government. We still have to work on and improve upon what we have, setting up the required institutions, because that is what our society needs, just as it needs special schools for other cases. In short, we must deal with this problem in the correct pedagogical and scientific manner.

But there are two fronts of the revolution, the fields in which the revolution has made the greatest gains, gains recognized all over the world, even by our enemies: education and public health, [*Applause*] in which the federation and women as a whole play a key role.

In the first place, the federation has made an effort to establish closer links between the school and the family: the dynamic Militant Mothers for Education movement—already a million, rather 1.4 million strong—carries out important, decisive tasks in education.* The federation is also involved in another very important institution, the school councils; and women participate in education, both in teaching and other educational activities as well as in the services required by each school, in which some 200,000 women are employed. Of the roughly 300,000 workers in education, about two-thirds are women.

What Third World, what Latin American country has reached our level of enrollment in school, in intermediate education? Which of these countries have reached the general education which our people are acquiring? This is chiefly due to the dedicated work of Cuban women.

When internationalism and the internationalist spirit of Cuban women were talked of here, two examples came to my mind: the Che Guevara Internationalist Detachment working in Angola, [*Applause*] made up of women in large measure, and one closer to home, the 1,200 Cuban teachers in Nicaragua, [*Applause*] who have helped open hundreds of classrooms and who went to work not in the cities but in the remotest regions of the country, some of which are a three-day journey on horseback; that's even more remote than the Sierra Maestra or Baracoa. In the sister country of Nicaragua there are less means of communication than in Cuba. They go to those areas to live like the peasant families who have taken them in, teaching children and adults, some of them have 50 students; others have 100 students and more, all in different grades. The news of the work they are doing and the

---

*The Militant Mothers for Education is a program composed mainly of housewives whose task is to check on students' attendance, help children in collective and individual study, help in the upkeep of the schools, sponsor Pioneer activities, and when appropriate, do substitute teaching. Over a million women participate.

prestige and recognition they have achieved in Nicaragua is impressive. Well, nearly half of them are women, nearly half! [*Applause*] And many of them are mothers. [*Applause*]

There were very few people who had to come back because they couldn't take it, very few. And I remember asking whether they were men or women. As far as I recall, there were no women in the first cases, not a single one. [*Applause*] There may have been some who returned for health reasons, but not because of the work.

Of course, when we promised our Sandinista brothers and sisters and the Nicaraguan people that we would send them doctors, health workers, and teachers, it was because we knew we had the necessary number of teachers, all that Nicaragua needed—1,200 and many more than that. We have over 30,000 students in the teacher-training schools alone and by this year all our teachers will be graduates. [*Applause*]

Remember that not so long ago 70 percent of our teachers weren't graduates. When schools were opened up all over to cope with the population boom, we didn't have enough graduate teachers for our schools. However, all the teachers we sent to Nicaragua are graduates with several years of experience.

Do you know how many teachers offered to go to Nicaragua? Twenty-nine thousand teachers offered their services; 29,000! [*Applause*] And about half were women. [*Applause*] This says a lot for our women because they are also mothers and wives. You really have to stop and think about what that means, the merit it represents and the awareness it shows.

We can't speak of awareness for its own sake and say we have great awareness. Sometimes we even complain of our lack of awareness for certain things; but when we speak of our people and their level of awareness, this is an example we must give; it is irrefutable proof.

I wonder where else in the hemisphere would such a thing have been possible. Where else could those 29,000 men and women be counted on? And this number was limited by the required standards of age and experience which were set. Well, I'm sure that Nicaragua will be able to count on such a force in the future—I have no doubt about it—Nicaragua will have such a force and will be able to help other peoples, [*Applause*] because the Nicaraguans are a people with exceptional virtues and heroism, who are now starting off on the path we started off on twenty years ago, the road to literacy. They have an illiteracy rate two-and-a-half times greater than what ours was. I think their illiteracy rate is about 70 percent. They plan to do away with illiteracy in a year, and their campaign starts on March 24. They will be mobilizing over 150,000 people to teach, and I'm sure that by the end of this year illiteracy will have been wiped out in Nicaragua and then it will be the second country in Latin America to have done so. [*Applause*] You see, nothing can be solved without the revolution, the second one!

They also have a high infant mortality rate: about 100 of every 1,000 children die in the first year, about 100. They will also reduce it considerably in the next few years. We are certain that other sister nations will have one day what we have today in terms of human and moral values.

This is also reflected in other areas, and although we are celebrating International Women's Day today and this is the conclusion of the women's congress, we can't forget other examples. At the time of the internationalist missions to Angola and Ethiopia, more than 300,000 Cubans were willing to participate, according to surveys that were made.*

When we speak of awareness, that is awareness in itself, that is proof; but of course we are still lacking in awareness with respect to many things, and we will have to develop it further.

Of course, even in those fields we have mentioned we aren't going to rest on our laurels, nor can we dream of past victories and gains, limiting ourselves to the present. No. We still are dissatisfied, very dissatisfied. We must do a great deal. We have been gaining in perfecting our teaching programs, but we must also make gains in terms of the experience of cadres who deal with children at all levels; in terms of organization and efficiency. We still have to overcome shortcomings in our system; revolutionaries cannot adopt any other stand. A conforming or self-satisfied position doesn't square with that of a revolutionary. I am talking about our people's effort.

There is another field, as I was saying, public health: a service which is so important, basic, and greatly appreciated by our people, in which most of the workers are women, including many women doctors. The participation of women in this field is tremendous.

So the women working in education and public health in our

*In November 1975, Cuba sent several thousand troops to Angola to stop a South African invasion of that country. In December 1977, Cuba began sending troops to Ethiopia in order to halt a U.S.-supported invasion by Somalia.

country number over 300,000, and the jobs are difficult. The work of a nurse is difficult; it is a task of great responsibility and importance. The federation also works directly in the field of health. The 61,000 health brigade members work on projects which are important for the family and for the people, preventing disease; for example, the vaccination programs against diptheria, whooping cough, tetanus, and others. In the Pap smear project there has been great progress and much more to come. Who knows how many thousands and maybe tens of thousands of lives have been saved by the Pap smear? This work by the masses in the health field will produce more miracles.

In the health field, in addition to the work of the FMC, there is the work of women as such, as workers. Here as well the results— although, I repeat, we shouldn't feel satisfied yet and must still overcome many shortcomings—the results are shown by the fact that in the year that has just ended our infant mortality rate dropped below 20—it was 19.4. [*Applause*]

What Third World country can compare its infant mortality figure with ours and with our life expectancy that is growing—I think it now stands at 69 years—and I think women live longer than men. [*Laughter*] Women live longer, but nobody can explain it, given the efforts and sacrifices they have to make; but it seems nature is wise. Isn't that the case? Don't women live longer? That's good news; [*Laughter and applause*] it shows that nature isn't so unjust.

Anyway, such great efforts have been put in to obtain that rate of 19.4! It's easy to say, but it required such an effort by doctors, nurses, and health workers; it required preventive medicine programs and prenatal care—women visit the doctor on an average of eight times before giving birth, as you noted in the report. It has required such an effort by maternity hospitals and doctors to constantly cut down the mortality rate—it has been a desperate struggle at times—and all along precise records have been kept.

Of course, that alone is an important achievement in the health field. I'm sure our Nicaraguan brothers and sisters will someday do likewise, cutting down on their present rate of 100; this will happen in the first years, because it is the elementary thing a people must do and if they haven't done it up until now it is the reactionary governments that are to blame. What did Somoza and his regime and the imperialists care about this issue?

If we're going to speak of the deaths for which imperialism is responsible, we'd have to mention the tens of thousands of children who died in Nicaragua from the time of the imperialists' first intervention to prevent Sandino's revolution.

If we were to estimate how many children and adults have died from neglect and lack of medical care over the past fifty years; when 100 out of every 1,000 die while it is possible to save 80 of those 100; it would really be noteworthy to estimate this figure. These are the data imperialism doesn't publish: the victims caused by its domination of the hemisphere, and when we speak of the hemisphere we must speak of millions upon millions because there are many countries with that infant mortality rate of 100 or 80, and some have a higher rate still. I don't know what the exact figure for Haiti is but I believe it's very high; there are some countries where it is higher than in Nicaragua; Brazil, with all its talk of industrial development, has areas where the rate is 200 and others where it is 100 or so, as a result of exploitation.

That is the legacy of capitalism, colonialism, neocolonialism, and imperialism, that's what it's shown by: that peoples are not masters of their country, of their destiny, and they are subjected to the most indolent governments, the most corrupt governments, the most submissive governments, and this gives rise to the great loss of human and moral values. And then the imperialists speak of human rights while they help starve to death millions of people with their system; they are simply crimes of the system!

In the two fields I mentioned women have played a decisive role.

One of the issues that was discussed the most while the main report was being drawn up—and it was discussed at the grass roots—one of the things that most concerns us has to do with the participation of women in the economy of the country. I want to discuss this and some of the concerns I know have cropped up on this subject.

There is no doubt that we have made great progress in this respect in the past years. This is shown, for example, by the fact that prior to the revolution there were 262,000 working women—I think that's the 1953 figure—and now there are 800,600. As Vilma explained in the report, it's not just a matter of numbers, but a change in the composition since formerly many of those jobs were as servants, in bars, and jobs of that sort to which women were relegated under capitalism. That is in contrast to the many skilled women now working: teachers, doctors, architects, nurses, intermediate technicians; 78,000 skilled women have joined the work force in the last few years. That alone shows the true nature of the change.

In the last five years some 200,000 women have started working, that is, women have joined the work force at a faster rate than men; that is logical because employment levels for men were higher. Now 30 percent of the work force consists of women.

In coming years it won't be easy for our country, for our revolution, to keep up that pace; for an underdeveloped country 30 percent is a high rate; of every 100, 30 women.

This comes at a time when the young people who made up the population boom are coming of work age. The boom made itself felt at the schools, in the efforts required to build elementary schools to cope, and then in the intermediate schools where we now have an enrollment of 1,100,000. When Fernández spoke here he said there had been an increase—I think he said fifteen times. [*Minister of Education José R. Fernández: "Twelve times."*] Twelve times, but if you said twelve you're wrong, Fernández, [*Laughter*] because there were only 70,000 and some; it doesn't make it—

He says there were 88,000. All right, twelve times, which is no small feat. One million one hundred thousand! Just think of what is required to cope with all the students we have. An enormous effort!

Now, we can't say that we are in a position to ensure—just as we guaranteed schools and medical care—increased jobs to keep pace with that growth, because it requires investments and new job opportunities. Therefore we will have some job problems as this enormous number of young people come of work age.

We feel that the revolution has the duty, the party and state have as their first duty doing all they can to come up with answers, with solutions to the employment problem.

This may also coincide with the quest for economic efficiency and productivity. It means savings in human resources, because efficiency in part means economizing on human resources. We are seeking greater efficiency. It is not a case of solving the problem by creating jobs per se, jobs which do not mean a service or benefit; putting fifty in an office to do work that can be done by twenty-five or thirty, for example. You understand what I mean. That wouldn't be the right solution and to create jobs based on inefficiency would be antieconomical.

We've been making an effort to raise productivity and have been achieving this; we've been making an effort for efficiency and have been achieving this; but we still have a lot to do, a lot to accomplish in this field. I recall there came a certain time when there weren't enough men in the Havana port to unload the boats, at a time when there was a flat rate, the same for loading five tons as for loading ten. In some jobs, linking work to wages has helped considerably in boosting productivity. There were never enough men around and the Havana port became a bottomless pit demanding more and more and more hands. And yet you have to see what has been achieved in productivity in the ports and in many other activities.

And so we now have greater efficiency, greater productivity, with a population explosion nearing work age.

It wouldn't be wise, it wouldn't be honest to make easy promises here, for we're very aware of what's needed in invest-ments to come up with an immediate answer to that mass of young men and women; the amount of economic resources that is required, and which we lack. And we can't say that in the next five years we'll be investing three times more, for we'll be investing only what we can invest. Now we must also think about the ways and means to provide useful employment. That's our duty. That's our responsibility. We must find them, and find them we will.

Recently at the National Assembly* a form of electricity payments, a form of monthly payment was discussed and recommended; it was asked that it be monthly and the conclusion was reached that it be monthly. Up to then it had been quarterly but calculated on a monthly average. The point was to go and take a reading and see exactly how much had been consumed each month, instead of going by averages. This requires a number—to take as an example—of persons to do the reading and collecting. Which won't be quarterly; what will be quarterly are your FMC dues. [*Laughter*] Monthly. And you know what a lot of walking is involved [*Laughter*] and how much our electric workers will have to walk. But this is necessary, the people are asking for it, it is considered more convenient. It generates a number of jobs, a job that can largely be done by women, and we mustn't forget that. [*Applause*] I give you this as an example.

And I can give you other examples. The textile industry is operating an average of 280 days every year, but it could operate 335 days a year and turn out more cloth on the basis of one more shift. An additional shift would mean the factory would not stop the week round. It would only stop for repairs during one period

*The National Assembly of People's Power is Cuba's highest state body.

of the year. And that would generate more jobs, jobs to be filled by women. This is just to give an example.

I can give you another. You know how it is in the sugar mills where the work is hard and goes on for 150 days. Someday we'll also have to consider ways in which the worker can rest during the harvest months, for it is very hard, very rough work. There'll come the time, when we've achieved greater efficiency, that this may be necessary. We haven't done so yet because there was a shortage of labor. Other things have been done to benefit the sugar worker; a basic step was to make the job a stable one. And this has been a demand dating back to the early years of the revolution, but we haven't been able to meet it. When things are a bit easier we'll be able to do some of these things. That is, it is possible to create more jobs in the factories we have now. Who knows how much can be done in small handicraft shops in terms of goods for home consumption and for export? Maybe the Sandinistas can help us on that score, because they have wonderful handicraft workers. Just look at the gift they brought for the federation today.

This is, of course, apart from the new factories now going into production. Recently, the Santa Clara textile plant started operations and this created jobs for thousands of people in Santa Clara. Right there the machine plant is being built, an important plant that will manufacture machinery for the sugar mills, such that the greater part of the components of a new sugar mill can be produced in Cuba. Now we're manufacturing nearly 50 percent and we'll be reaching 70 percent. We will be turning out complete tandems. Two big cement plants will begin production this year. And there are other new plants we've been building that will be going into production. There are new industrial investment programs services which will be developed.

Naturally, sometimes the problem we run into is that jobs are not evenly distributed. There are places where we need workers now, where there won't be enough and in other places we have a surplus. It is in eastern Cuba that we have the problem of the greatest surplus, because, to go back to the population explosion, the explosion was greatest in the eastern provinces; the number of births there far exceeded that of the western provinces, for instance. The western provinces can't and shouldn't emulate with the eastern provinces where population is concerned. [*Laughter*] In some areas we have problems of more workers than jobs available. But when the time comes to develop an area like Moa, personnel has to be brought in from all over the country. There are thousands and thousands of builders from all the country in Moa. When the times comes to build more in Cienfuegos, now that we have to build the first atomic power plant, many thousands will have to work there. When we start building the steel plant on the north coast of eastern Cuba, we will also have to mobilize thousands and thousands of construction workers.

So the problem that presents itself is a real, objective one, but this does not exonerate us in any way from the sacred, elementary duty of searching for formulas to solve the employment problem, and in this, as regards women, we've been making a good deal of progress.

But, mind you, no matter what, in all that we have made progress, what we have to avoid is falling back in any way. That's very important! [*Applause*] That there be no falling off of that 30 percent; and if it's possible to advance some, we will advance as far as reality permits.

Needless to say, in the developed socialist countries this percentage is higher, some 40 percent and more. But this is not yet our case.

We have to go carefully and analyze this problem well.

Of course, we are decidedly in favor of having preferential posts for women in workplaces, decidedly in favor. I think we should keep that up.

I know that other questions have been discussed here, related, for example, to some jobs which are not authorized for women. That's a different kind of problem because, let's say, it is a medical problem, a health problem; you just can't take any decision on a problem of this nature. It can, however, be brought up for review, because as technology is developed and more equipment used, as work conditions change, the number of jobs women can't fill now will be fewer and fewer. See how in many activities already, in construction, for instance, women are taking an increasing part; in the sugar mills there are more and more women.

So these jobs to which women have no access are on the decrease, as the conditions of production are changing.

In my opinion the fact that management can freely take on workers* does not prevent them from consulting with organiza-

---

*Prior to 1980, all hiring of workers in Cuba was centrally administered. The new system put into effect enabled the various state enterprises to hire workers directly.

tions, consulting with trade unions, consulting with the [women's] federation [*Applause*] during the selection process for personnel to be taken on directly by the enterprise, for it's not a matter of placing an ad in the paper, of going about it secretly. To hire somebody you must know who you're hiring, who you're selecting.

There might be two cases: two women who offer the same but one has family income problems while the other doesn't. The case could arise. And this must be borne in mind. [*Applause*] We can't go just by a strictly economic criterion, without ever taking into account a question of social justice. We're not capitalists; we're socialists, and we want to be communists. [*Applause*] And I think that would help; it doesn't have to be an obstacle.

Direct hiring of workers means that there be no more central-ized allocation of the work force, but it doesn't mean that the manager is accordingly given complete free rein. I think that the practical, useful thing is for the manager to consult: with the trade union, the [women's] federation. I think that would help in making the best selection of personnel, of this I haven't the slightest doubt, without violating the principle of direct hire.

I think we must be very careful in that certain situations do not lead us to retrace our steps in what we have gained for women, which is a lot. We must consolidate this and progress more.

If we analyze the number of women who are studying, particu-larly in many of these activities, like teachers, nurses, middle-level technicians in the health sector, and in general, those studying in the universities, where there's a high percentage of women, there's no doubt that there will continue to be a consider-able increase in women's skills and their potential access to many technical jobs. Many women comrades are distinguishing themselves in this respect.

I believe you appointed today to the National Committee a distinguished woman comrade who heads a research center, who in the past and at this very moment is directing work to combat African swine fever. And more and more women are earning a place for themselves in technical jobs. The outlook on that front is positive.

I was saying that we had to be careful not to fall back on what we have achieved so far, for we've had to work very hard and struggle very hard against incomprehension and prejudice to bring about a climate of equality, to overcome prejudice, back-ward ways of thinking. And, of course, if we fall back as regards jobs, if we fall back in the economic field, we will start going back on everything else we've gained.

And I sincerely think that it is our duty, the duty of the party, the duty of the state, the duty of the trade unions, to concern ourselves over this, and the duty also of the women. It is one of the tasks, the functions, the goals, of the federation, which is not just working for the revolution, not just helping in the health field, in education, in the fight against crime, in all the tasks in which women participate. Not only does the federation play a very important role in economic tasks and in the services; it also has the duty to pay close attention to all the questions that concern women, that are of interest to women, and to defend those interests in the party and in the state.

See how you yourselves have come up with some solutions. Some time ago, whenever a meeting of the light industry sector was held, the workers there—and many of them are women— invariably raised the problem of schools and complained that the schools closed at 4:30 p.m., and that day-care centers closed at such and such a time and that Saturday mornings were a headache, and you yourselves began to come up with the solutions, with the idea of teachers' aides.

Today there is talk—although in some provinces there are still some basic problems, it would seem from what has been said here—of a better selection of teachers' aides. But you yourselves thought up solutions to the problem, because there really was a contradiction between the time school was over and the time you finished work; you started seeking formulas. And now you've been discussing not the problem but how the solution which you found is coming along.

In the same way, the federation must strive to think of everything that can help in terms of the job situation and solving all the problems you have raised here. And this is very important; it's one of the tasks the Federation of Cuban Women must pay attention to, in connection with the problem of jobs I'm talking about and in taking part in the economic life of the country, although, realistically speaking, we can't continue with the same growth rate as over past years for the reasons we have explained.

New sources of employment are opening up. We already have thousands of men and women comrades, for instance, working in other countries, obtaining skills. We have several thousand in the GDR [German Democratic Republic—East Germany] and Czechoslovakia; we have thousands of comrades working abroad as technicians—thousands!—or as construction workers. Of course, in these types of activities—I don't know whether I'll be accused of discriminating—if we have to send ten thousand builders, then logically, because of the kind of work involved, most of them will be men. And so we can send men primarily for some of these activities, since women are sometimes discriminated against. They don't want them sometimes in war, they just don't want them, in spite of the fact that they have shown their ability to participate. [*Applause*]

If there are openings for the nation to engage in overseas work of an economic nature, we can use our reserve of men, without excluding the women of course, without excluding them; but we're aware that when women must leave the family behind, the human sacrifice is greater than when a man leaves. We're aware of that.

We all have the duty of seeking out wise, just solutions to these problems. And you can trust in the party, for this will be the line the party follows.

There's been plenty of talk here about the promotion of women in political and administrative posts. I think this subject is still of the greatest importance. In some fields we have fallen back. For instance, in the People's Power elections fewer women were elected in the second election than in the first election. There were fewer women the second time round. In the National Assembly there was a good proportion, but in the grass-roots elections, in the circumscriptions, there were fewer than in the last elections. This, naturally, must give us food for thought and cause for concern, the way we have fallen back, especially when we were complaining about the results of the first. We were hoping for progress and instead we fell back.

Of course, there are some explanations that can be given; some were given here, the many responsibilities women still have, how difficult things become. But, isn't there some prejudice too? Isn't there some prejudice, even among the women who go to the polls and vote prejudiced? I'm not saying that women must be voted for just because they're women. When one goes to the polls, the vote should be given to whoever, in the citizen's opinion, is better prepared, and better qualified; but no one should not vote for a woman because she happens to be a woman or through prejudice. All the same, I think that the percentage of women elected in the People's Power elections, in the grass-roots elections, is really low.

In other fields we have progressed. It was said here, for instance, how women constitute more than 40 percent of the trade union leaders. I think that when the last congress was held the figure was less, some 30 percent. That is, it's remarkable how women have gone from making up some 30 percent to over 40 percent of the trade union leadership. This speaks highly of how our workers have confidence in women.

I wasn't able to personally hear Comrade Landy's speech, but I was told later that he mentioned some figures, on the situation in the Young Communist League, on how women already make up 40 percent of the membership. They jumped from 29 to 40 percent. I think this is a meaningful jump. We've advanced in the party. We've already reached 18.9. I understand that, for instance, in the Federation of Students of Intermediate Education, 65 percent of the leaders are young women. In the Pioneer organization—and perhaps this is what is most promising—girls hold 75 percent of the positions of responsibility, 75 percent! [*Applause*] Remarkable! You can see the children are not prejudiced; [*Laughter*] when they're going to choose, they choose girls. I think this is really promising and interesting.

But neither the party nor the government can give up—they can't give up for a second—the struggle on behalf of the advancement of women. I am absolutely convinced that society stands to gain insofar as it is able to develop and make use of the moral, human, and intellectual qualities and capabilities of women. I'm absolutely convinced of this. And this is precisely what sets a just society, a socialist society, apart from a capitalist one.

But I'm by no means convinced that the idea of equality has even triumphed on a world scale. There aren't many examples. And I'm including the socialist countries. I think women should be promoted more at the state and party level, I honestly do. [*Applause*]

It is our duty to create the conditions to develop that awareness. It is our duty, our moral obligation, and all the more so when I think that our party is still largely a party of men, and our state is still largely a state of men. Perhaps here on the platform we don't have a majority supporting that thesis. [*Laughter*] I'm looking at some male comrades and I don't know what they think. But I really believe this. And I say aren't we still prejudiced no matter how much we declare war on those prejudices?

That is another very important theme taken up at this congress, in the main report and in the theses. As I said, we have progressed but we still have a long way to go and we have to prevent any falling back in this historic—and it is historic—struggle.

Various problems affecting women, especially regarding the services, were dealt with at the congress. In promoting equality we have clearly progressed institutionally, with the Family Code, the Code on [Children and] Youth, and the constitution. We have progressed juridically, but we have to progress in practice too. What constitutes an unfair burden for women? What can alleviate that burden? And that's why problems with services reflect always, especially on women workers, and why they have been brought up. I really have my doubts as to whether we are going about things in the right way. When the hairdressers close at such and such an hour, that's that. And then the working woman can't go to the hairdresser. [*Applause*] I give one example, the hairdressers, which is by no means the most basic. But the problem of laundries was raised here also.

So this has been put forward, and put forward strongly. The stores were brought up. I know, at least in the report it says that when they stopped [special opening hours]—[*Applause*] It says in the main report that that was a step backwards and that when some experiments they were doing were stopped the federation wasn't consulted at all; it wasn't asked for its opinion. [*Applause*] It says that in the main report.

I think we should reflect on whether we aren't able to solve such problems. We started out trying to solve the problem of the schools by bringing in teachers' aides. Why can't hairdressers be open after normal work hours? [*Applause*] Don't bus workers work at night? Don't doctors and nurses and other hospital staff work at night? [*Applause*] Don't electrical workers work at night keeping up output at peak hours? [*Applause*] Because if it really—? Because even if fewer people go it does mean more time for people, even those not working: what there does seem to be is a need for it.

And of course what Vilma said in the report I've heard too: that absenteeism, authorization to receive those services during work hours, has practically been legalized. It has been legalized, [*Applause*] because there's no way of solving those problems any other time; they have to be solved during work hours. And, listen, there are 800,000 women working, 800,600 according to the figures.

If they have those problems why can't we think up other, more reasonable solutions? Services that do function at other hours.

And haven't we been saying that we're going to have some
employment problems? Well, that means more jobs in the hairdressers and other centers, more jobs. [*Applause*]

The formulas can vary: opening hours can vary, there can be
more shifts, it depends on what it is and what is most advisable.
Because the point is that if they don't go to the hairdressers
they'll be doing their hair at home, and if they do go to the
hairdressers they'll be paying for the service they receive. And
not all the employees have to be there, as say, during peak hours.
The whole staff doesn't have to be around at 8:00 or 9:00 at night.
There can be just one or two. That'll have to be studied. And why
can't the laundries be working at night, if it's a service that's
being paid for? [*Applause*] People are going to pay for that
service; they're going to pay for it!

We have to think up practical solutions. We don't have to be
dogmatic, inflexible about it. We must do things that will help
people with their problems; we understand that.

I haven't yet heard a single man, let me tell you, protest about
that. [*Laughter*] Not a single one! [*Applause*] And there must be
some reason! Despite the [family] code! [*Laughter*] They are
arguments being put forward by women workers, basically, and
they have to do with a reality. It's being said all over the place.
Why shouldn't we be open to looking for other solutions and
providing useful services? I am talking about a service that is
useful to the population, services that are paid for. And that's a
reality.

I believe that the comrades in charge of these fronts should
analyze such issues more carefully and come up with reasonable,
fair solutions to these problems: they should help create the
conditions so that women workers don't go out of their minds.

The report, the congress, and the theses have patently shown
the internationalist spirit of Cuban women. Our federation has
really taken on a lot of important internationalist work in the
WIDF [Women's International Democratic Federation], and also
in the United Nations, with International Women's Year and the
International Year of the Child. It must be said, and we say it
with satisfaction, that the federation has earned a great deal of
prestige internationally, [*Applause*] in international bodies, in
women's organizations in other countries—countries of both the
socialist camp and the capitalist camp—liberation movement
organizations and organizations of underdeveloped countries. It
has gained a lot of well-deserved prestige. I think that our

federation has contributed enormously to the foreign policy of the revolution. [*Applause*]

The school that I mentioned is proof of confidence in the revolution. I believe that the women comrades of Namibia, of South Africa, of liberation movements, our Saharan women comrades, have students here in the FMC's national school for cadres; there are dozens and dozens of students from all over. This is an important international service we are providing: helping train cadres for women's organizations in countries where there are liberation movements and Third World countries that need them. And I think it's highly significant that two-thirds of the students are from other countries, are foreigners—I say foreigners, but to us none of the delegations here, none of the students from Namibia or South Africa, are foreigners. They are our brothers and sisters. [*Applause*]

The federation takes an active part in the international women's movement but also in the international revolutionary movement and in international solidarity. And we are reassured by the knowledge that when the party, when the country has offered something, it can meet its commitment. It can do so because ours are a people who meet their commitments, in whom one can trust. [*Applause*]

Allow me to say a few words about the international situation.

In the last few weeks, the international situation has become worse. There has been a significant step backward in the gains made in handling the arms race, promoting international détente and the search for peace as a result of imperialist policy, of the actions of the most reactionary imperialist elements that have made the situation worse as of a few months ago.

You will recall the hue and cry that went up at the time of the Sixth Summit regarding the presence of Soviet military personnel in Cuba, personnel that had been in Cuba for seventeen years.* All the U.S. administrations knew about it, everybody knew about it. However, they started a campaign and mounted a big scandal around this issue to justify their hostile policy toward

---

*The Sixth Summit Conference of the Movement of Nonaligned Countries was held September 1979 in Havana, attended by representatives from 138 countries. Around the same time, the U.S. government launched an international propaganda campaign around the existence of a "Soviet combat brigade" in Cuba, referring to training personnel that had been in Cuba since the early 1960s.

Cuba, to combat Cuba's influence, and also to justify interventionist moves in the area and to delay the ratification of SALT II.

After that, they renewed their spy flights over our country; they organized a task force in the Key West area, a military task force; they organized some landings in Guantánamo Bay. That's with regard to our country.

Internationally, they moved to set up military bases in the Indian Ocean; they used the events in Iran as an excuse to send naval squads to the Indian Ocean and Persian Gulf area. In NATO they agreed to deploy 572 medium-range nuclear missiles in Europe, trying to change the balance of forces and obtain the upper hand militarily. What's more, the imperialists took advantage of the events in Afghanistan, which they themselves provoked with their intervention from abroad, to increase international tensions to the utmost; to approve big military budgets and spending; to continue on the path of setting up bases to try to upset the balance of forces; to plunge the world into the cold war era once again; to justify the aggressive policy of imperialism all over the world.

Naturally, all these developments are cause for concern, because such situations of international tension affect everybody, and now the world is faced with a series of crises: economic, energy, inflation, recession. What might the consequences be if we add a return to the cold war accompanied by an upsurge in the arms race, as far as the peoples of the world are concerned, as regards all peoples without exception? All these problems are extremely serious, especially for the underdeveloped countries. At a time when we must struggle most for peace and international cooperation, at a time when we must mobilize economic resources for the development of many countries—which is what we proposed at the UN—this really serious and worrisome situation for all peoples of the world has arisen.

We wonder if the world can afford to embark on a new arms race and a cold war, given its economic problems.

The arms expenditures which Vilma mentioned in the final resolution already come to more than 400 billion dollars a year— 400 billion dollars a year! It's truly incredible amidst the economic problems and poverty that affect billions of people. It is madness.

The present situation also affects us.

Recently Carter's main adviser said that, if there was a problem in any other area of the world, they would decide the area which was most convenient for maneuvering. The Washington observers feel that he meant Cuba, that he had Cuba in mind. Nobody in the U.S. government denied it, by the way. It was a clear threat to our country, implying that if a conflict broke out in the Persian Gulf they would respond by attacking us.

Of course, to attack us they must reckon with us, they must also take us into account! [*Applause and shouts of "For sure, Fidel, give the Yankees hell!"*] This shows that the imperialists just don't learn the lessons of history. I think that this is a shameful way to threaten our country. They have forgotten about prior problems, the problems which gave rise to the October Crisis and which were at the root of the crisis, and the measures Cuba adopted because of the threat of an invasion.

Of course we aren't going to get nervous. [*Shouts of "Never!"*] Twenty-one years of revolution have passed, and the imperialists' threats have yet to cause us sleepless nights. The danger? We know that we have lived with danger; we know the price of our revolution. We have had to live with twenty-one years of danger, yes indeed. Sometimes the danger has been greater, sometimes less, depending on the president, his advisers, and other factors. That was a clear reference to Cuba.

What's more, they are encouraging illegal departures from the country and the seizure of boats. They all but give those who seize boats a hero's welcome. There have been several cases, and we have protested to them and warned them. The last time some people drowned on the journey, but we said, "It isn't our fault since we didn't impose the restrictions." We have asked and demanded that they take measures to discourage that sort of thing because all the consequences are well known.

That was how the hijackings started, and then there was no way of stopping the flood of planes that were hijacked and brought here from the United States; while it's true that there are lunatics everywhere, there are many more there than here. [*Applause*] There were times when there were three U.S. planes here. Then I imagine that they won't have the nerve to demand that we take measures—as we are doing—against plane hijackers; if they don't act against those who hijack boats. [*Applause*]

We also trust they will take measures to discourage illegal departures from the country; otherwise we would also have to take measures. We did so once, but we aren't going to take measures against those who want to leave illegally while they're being encouraged by the imperialists. We were compelled to take measures once. We have also warned them, because we had to open up the port of Camarioca once.* We think it shows lack of maturity on the part of the United States to create similar situations once again, because we hold the view that this revolutionary association is voluntary, voluntary! [*Applause*] The struggle for socialism and communism is a voluntary one: that was, is, and will be our view. So I trust we won't be forced to take such measures again. They shouldn't feel that we don't have answers to their policies.

The United States's plans for intervention everywhere, but especially in this area, are evident in the Caribbean and Central America. They are planning to intervene in Grenada, Nicaragua, El Salvador, Cuba; the Caribbean and Central America. Their plans for intervention to contain the revolutionary movement are very clear.

They tried it in Nicaragua and encountered strong resistance from the nations of Latin America. They are maneuvering to foil the revolutionary process in El Salvador as well. Their intentions are clear, they're evident. However, this won't stop the process of the people's drive to obtain independence in this hemisphere. In one way or the other, on one path or the other, the peoples must move towards independence and have the chance of doing what we have done and what the Nicaraguans have done or are doing.

Women from Canada, the United States, France, Spain have spoken here and explained the problems they have, the social problems, the situation of women in those countries, how they are subjected to discrimination and injustice; I heard them speak here from this tribune.

Why? Why shouldn't the peoples of our continent have the right to freedom and independence? There were too many centuries of colonial and imperialist oppression, and it simply wasn't going to last forever. It can't last forever. They will have to give up their imperialist policies, their policy of intervention in this hemisphere. They will have to renounce that and resign themselves to the reality that the peoples of Latin America and the Caribbean

*Following an initial wave of Cuban emigration to the U.S. in the early 1960s, Washington began to shut the door, hoping to build up discontent within Cuba. In response, the revolutionary government opened up the port of Camarioca for U.S. ships to come and pick up those wanting to leave. In response to a similar situation, in which the U.S. government closed off legal emigration while encouraging illegal departures, Cuba opened up the port of Mariel in April 1980. Over 100,000 Cubans left, many of them tempted by the greater availability of consumer goods in the United States.

have the right to be free, to be the masters of their own destinies and to make the changes they deem necessary, because they will never be able to prevent it.

They might well create a colossal Vietnam in this hemisphere; if they try to hold things back, they'll create a colossal Vietnam in Central America, or bigger still, in the hemisphere; because they will not be able to brake the peoples' struggle, the peoples will not be intimidated, no people ever will. Revolutionaries have not been afraid for a long time now, and the Sandinistas proved that; [*Applause*] the Sandinistas proved that in a heroic, impressive way, and now the Salvadorans are proving it in their heroic, impressive way. [*Applause*]

And nothing can stop that spirit. They can make the struggle costlier, they can make it bloodier and more painful, but there's no way they can prevent it. They could still have the historical sense of what's inevitable being inevitable and resign themselves to the reality that our peoples seek to become, and will never stop until they have become, absolutely independent and free, the masters of their own destinies.

Yes, one must have a sense of history to know what that means, what revolution means here, next to the imperialist monster; yes, what the Cuban revolution and its firm, unwavering line has meant. One needs a sense of history and of realities to understand the merit of the Sandinista revolution, the merit of the Grenadian revolution. Grenada, Nicaragua, and Cuba are three giants rising up to defend their right to independence, sovereignty, and justice, on the very threshold of imperialism. [*Applause*]

Only the peoples who are capable of doing that can be called giants. And the number of giants will inevitably grow until the day when our America is a giant, [*Applause*] and then, if you wish, there will be two giants: them and our peoples. [*Applause*] But we have a right to live, we have a right to develop, we have a right to justice, we have a right to progress! And not the way it's been up to now, when we've been treated in the most miserable and abject manner imaginable. The way they did last century with Mexico and with Central America, and with the Caribbean, and with the whole of Latin America. And we know there are risks. In the face of the threats and insinuations as to our being victim to invasions, we shall respond by strengthening our defenses [*Applause*] and furthering our awareness, [*Applause*] we shall respond as we have always responded in the past. [*Applause*]

We regret this should be so, because it will take a long time for them to understand these realities, to resign themselves to the reality of Cuba, to resign themselves to the realities of today's world. We'll have to wait a long time for that.

There's something we're certain of. We've spent twenty years in these conditions, twenty-one. And twenty-one years is a long time: twenty-one years of the blockade; twenty-one years of threats against Cuba; twenty-one years of them not resigning themselves to Cuba. And now I don't know whether they're getting nervous as they watch other peoples follow the road to independence and the road to revolution, to their own revolution, not the Cuban revolution. People make their own revolution, in their own way. We made it our way, the Nicaraguans, their way, the Grenadians, theirs. And each new revolution makes a new contribution to revolutionary experience. The Sandinistas are making their contribution, the Grenadians are making theirs. What characterizes us is precisely our own spirit of independence; what characterizes us is the defense of our countries' sovereign principles, our peoples' desire to fight, to wipe out illiteracy, poverty, and unemployment, the lack of medical attention, indignity. And there was plenty enough of this in our country, including prostitution, gambling, the drug traffic. All these indignities our people wiped out, as other peoples are doing now. And, I repeat, it's going to take a good long time. We must be prepared for it taking a long time. I'm convinced of that.

This does not mean that we should give up our struggle for peace. We do not follow a policy of provocations; we're not interested in creating conflicts; we're aware that it is our country's duty to fight for peace, to do its part in helping to prevent the international situation from becoming worse, to prevent the return of the cold war. We're aware that this is one of our duties, not only as an independent country, an aware country, a revolutionary country, a socialist country, but also as a country that has a responsibility toward other countries in the Non-aligned movement. We know of the world's problems; we know how necessary it is to insist on the quest for peace, on international cooperation, on the solution to economic problems, to developmental problems of the world. We know this is our duty, our obligation, and we will not give up the fight. We will not give up fighting for that. We will not give up making an international contribution in the struggle for peace, in the struggle for détente; that is, we will not give up making these efforts. It is our duty to make them. But we must be realistic, for it isn't enough that we follow one international policy while another type of policy is being used against us. We can't move from this hemisphere. And even if we could, we wouldn't, as a matter of honor and dignity. [*Prolonged applause*] We're really satisfied with our geographic location.

We're not following a deliberate head-on policy as regards the United States. We're not even reluctant to talk; we are not against making an effort to improve relations, if this in any way helps bring about a climate of peace in the hemisphere or in the international arena. In other words, it's good that we set forth our policy so that nobody can get us wrong, so that there's no room for mistakes. But we can indeed guarantee and assure everybody, our adversaries, that this country can never be threatened, can never be intimidated, can never be made to acquiesce, can never be forced to give up a single one of its principles. [*Prolonged applause and shouts of "There are no two Fidels and there are no two Cubas!"*]

This year our party will hold its second congress.* This year we'll be drawing up a second five-year plan, with a lot more organization and experience, aware of the difficulties and the limitations; but we will not become discouraged and neither are we going to fail to make our best effort. Relying on our own resources, relying on solidarity and economic relations with the socialist camp. With or without the blockade, we'll go on fighting against all the difficulties, [*Applause*] against them all! The difficulties of nature and difficulties of all kinds. They'll never succeed in discouraging anyone in the ranks of the revolution. [*Applause*]

This year is a year of difficulties, but it will also be a year of progress, progress in everything that it is in our hands to improve, everything that is still to be improved subjectively, as in the example of the buses and many others. As evidenced by the efforts being made by those who are getting the soil ready at this moment, that tremendous effort we know so well. [*Applause*] And the effort I'm certain our people will make in these two months, and the two others as well, to face up to the difficulties as they should be faced, with the right amount of energy and the right courage and determination. It'll be a year of difficulties but also a year of progress in many fields, one in which the revolution will come out politically and ideologically strengthened.

*The Second Congress of the Communist Party of Cuba was held December 17-20, 1980, in Havana.

The outlook for the second party congress is magnificent and cause for great happiness. Party members are more seasoned, better prepared, more in number—both the party and the Young Communist League. It is also highly encouraging to have witnessed this congress, very encouraging. [*Applause*] It's very encouraging for our party and for all of us, the quality of this congress, the depth of this congress, the spirit reflected in this congress, for we know you're from the grass-roots level and you come from all corners of the country. [*Applause*] You've brought here the energy, the revolutionary enthusiasm, the revolutionary awareness from all corners of our country; [*Applause*] you've brought here the maturity of our revolution, you've brought here the experience of our revolution. [*Applause*]

And we have other mass organizations as powerful as the federation; our glorious labor movement; [*Applause*] our Committees for the Defense of the Revolution that celebrate their twentieth anniversary this year; [*Applause*] our peasant movement; [*Applause*] our student organizations; [*Applause*] our Pioneer organization; [*Applause*] our Young Communist League; [*Applause*] our party. [*Prolonged applause*]

That's what we're counting on to face the future! That's what we're counting on to continue the march ahead, to go on deepening and strengthening our revolution, and to continue putting our internationalist principles into practice in a fitting way! [*Applause*]

Thank you, comrades! Thank you for the encouragement this congress has given us, for the encouragement we have received from you!

Patria o muerte!

Venceremos! [*Ovation*]

APPENDIX A

Maternity Law for Working Women

Official translation of the Cuban Ministry of Justice.

Executive Branch, Council of Ministers

I, OSVALDO DORTICÓS TORRADO, president of the Republic of Cuba,

HEREBY PROCLAIM: That the Council of Ministers has approved and I have signed the following:

WHEREAS: Studies made on problems pertaining to working women, especially those relating to maternity, counsel the enactment of new legislation in order to grant the maximum guarantee to all maternity rights which, although recognized and provided for by Social Security Law No. 1100 of March 27, 1963, should be reconsidered on the basis of present-day medical and scientific principles.

WHEREAS: It is a primary interest of the revolutionary government to give special attention to the working mother since, in addition to her valuable contribution to society in the procreation and education of children, she also fulfills her social duty by working.

WHEREAS: A successful pregnancy as well as the delivery and the future health of the child require the adoption of adequate measures on the part of the pregnant woman, as an unavoidable duty toward her child and society.

WHEREAS: To secure the above-mentioned measures, it is necessary to ensure medical attention and rest to the working woman during her pregnancy, the breast-feeding of the newborn during the first months of life which will protect it from disease and favor the development of strong emotional bonds between mother and child, and the systematic medical examination of the child by a pediatrician during its first year of life.

WHEREAS: In our country all medical and hospital services, including pharmaceutical and hospital dietary services related to maternity are guaranteed free of charge to all the population. This makes it necessary to establish additional legislation on the enjoyment of said rights by the working woman or the wife or the companion of a worker.

THEREFORE: By virtue of the authority vested in them, the Council of Ministers resolves to dictate the following:

LAW NO. 1263
MATERNITY LAW FOR WORKING WOMEN

Chapter 1: Scope and Protection

Article 1. The present law comprises the working woman and protects her maternity, guaranteeing and facilitating, in a special manner, her medical attention during pregnancy, her rest before and after delivery, the breast-feeding and care of the children, as well as a financial aid in those cases specified in these provisions.

Chapter 2: Paid Leave

Article 2. Every pregnant working woman, regardless of type of work, will be obliged to stop working on the thirty-fourth week of pregnancy and will have the right to a leave of absence of eighteen weeks, which will include six weeks before delivery and twelve weeks after delivery. This leave will be paid as determined by this law, provided that the working woman meets the requirements stated in Article 11.

The Ministry of Labor, at the proposal of the Central Organization of Cuban Trade Unions, will regulate exceptional situations in those places of work whose special characteristics, according to medical and scientific criteria, make it necessary that working women take prenatal leave for longer periods than those established by this law.

Article 3. In cases of multiple pregnancy, the working woman will be obliged to stop working on the thirty-second week of pregnancy, extending to eight weeks the period of her paid leave before delivery.

Article 4. If delivery does not take place during the period established for the prenatal leave, this leave will be extended to the date on which delivery takes place and the extended time period will be paid for up to two weeks.

Article 5. If delivery takes place before the expiration of the prenatal leave, this leave will cease and the working woman will begin her postnatal leave.

Article 6. If delivery takes place before the thirty-fourth week of pregnancy, or before the thirty-second week in the case of multiple pregnancy, the leave will include only the postnatal period.

Article 7. The working woman will be guaranteed a postnatal leave of six weeks necessary for her recovery, even when, because of adverse circumstances of accident or acquired or congenital diseases, the child dies at birth or during the first four weeks after birth.

Article 8. If the working woman, because of complications during delivery, requires a longer period of recovery beyond the postnatal leave, she will have the right to receive the subsidy for illness as established in the Social Security Law.

Chapter 3: Accidents of Pregnancy

Article 9. Accidents of pregnancy are those complications relative to pregnancy or diseases acquired during pregnancy which require absolute bed rest by doctor's order, with or without hospitalization.

Accidents of pregnancy which occur before the thirty-fourth week will give the working woman the right to subsidy for illness as established in the Social Security Law.

Chapter 4: Financial Aid

Article 10. The financial aid that the working woman will receive during her maternity leave will be equal to the weekly average of salaries and subsidies she has received during the twelve months immediately prior to the leave. This aid will never be under ten pesos a week.

Article 11. In order to have the right to receive the paid maternity leave established by this law, it will be indispensable that the working woman have her records in order, exception made in the case of administrative negligence, and have worked not less than seventy-five days in the twelve months immediately prior to the leave. However, even when the working woman does not fulfill these requirements, she will have the right to receive the complementary leaves established in the following chapter.

Chapter 5: Complementary Maternity Leave

Article 12. During pregnancy and up to the thirty-fourth week, the working woman will have the right to six days or twelve half-days of paid leave for her medical and dental care prior to delivery.

Article 13. In order to guarantee the care and development of the child during the first year of life; the working woman will have the right every month to one day off, with pay, to take her child for a pediatric check-up.

Chapter 6: Unpaid Leave

Article 14. The working mother will have the right to an unpaid leave for the purpose of taking care of her children, under the terms and conditions established by this law.

Interim Provisions

First: The present law will be applied to all working women who, at the time of its promulgation, have fulfilled thirty-four weeks of pregnancy and have still not taken their maternity leave, and to those who are already on leave according to Social Security Law No. 1100 of March 27, 1963, as regards the extension of the leave to twelve weeks after delivery and one day off, with pay, every month for pediatric visits. Additional payment to cover the extended postnatal leave will be given as established in this law.

Second: The extra hour of rest period for child care established by Law No. 1100 of March 27, 1963, will remain for those working women now enjoying this benefit.

Third: Working women enjoying unpaid leave, as established in Instruction No. 1 of the Labor Justice Office of the Ministry of Labor, dated September 23, 1968, will maintain the same labor rights established in said instruction, until the expiration of their leave.

Final Provisions

First: The Ministry of Labor is authorized to dictate as many provisions as required for the execution and application of this law.

Second: Title II of Law No. 1100 of March 27, 1963, Instruction No. 1 of the Labor Justice Office of the Ministry of Labor dated September 23, 1968, and all other provisions and rulings which oppose the fulfillment of this law, are hereby abrogated. This law will go into effect on the date of its promulgation in the *Official Gazette of the Republic.*

THEREFORE: I command that this law be fulfilled and enforced in all its parts.

SIGNED, at the Palace of the Revolution, in Havana, on January 14, 1974.

OSVALDO DORTICÓS TORRADO

Fidel Castro Ruz
Prime Minister
Oscar Fernández Padilla
Minister of Labor

Regulations of Law 1263
Ministry of Labor, Resolution No. 2

WHEREAS: Law No. 1263 of January 14, 1974, in the first final provisions authorizes the passing of as many provisions as required for the execution and enforcement of said law.

THEREFORE: By virtue of the authority vested in me,

I RESOLVE:

FIRST: To dictate for the execution and enforcement of Law No. 1263 of January 14, 1974, the following:

Regulations

Responsibility of the Administration in Workplaces

Article 1. The administration in all workplaces will be responsible for payments of all financial aid stipulated in Law No. 1263 of January 14, 1974.

Article 2. The administration will have the obligation of granting maternity leave after the thirty-fourth week of pregnancy—or after the thirty-second week of pregnancy in case of multiple births—once the working woman presents the medical certificate required.

Article 3. The fulfillment of the paid leave stipulated in Articles 2 and 7 of the law will take place in three parts: The first, at the beginning of the prenatal leave; the second, at the beginning of the first six weeks of the postnatal leave; and the third, at the beginning of the last six weeks of the postnatal leave, when applicable.

Article 4. In exceptional cases when delivery does not take place within the six-week period of the prenatal leave, the said leave will be extended until delivery actually takes place; payment for the additional period will never be over a term of two weeks, after which it will be considered an unpaid leave.

Article 5. The payment of two weeks stipulated in the preceding article will be made jointly with the payment of the six weeks of the postnatal leave.

Article 6. If delivery takes place before the expiration of the prenatal leave, the financial difference between this date and the original expiration of the leave will be deducted from the postnatal leave, as stipulated in Article 5 of the law.

Article 7. In order to grant the rights stipulated by the law, the administration will be responsible in all cases to demand the medical certificates or assistance notes to medical services issued by establishments of the Ministry of Public Health.

Article 8. The administration will have the obligation to guarantee that the working woman who resumes her work upon expiration of the maternity leave will have the right to occupy the same post she had before.

The Amount of Payment

Article 9. In order to calculate the average weekly income, referred in Article 10 of the law, the salaries and subsidies received by the working woman during the twelve months immediately prior to the start of the maternity leave, will be added up and its result divided by fifty-two weeks.

Article 10. The procedure to calculate the amount of payment established in the previous article will be applied in all cases, including those working women with a work record of less than one year. Trial periods in the case of new workers will be included for the purpose of calculation.

Article 11. A temporary working woman with a work record will have the right to a paid maternity leave and receive the payment even when the start of the same does not coincide with her cycle of work. The amount of payment will be calculated in the same way as for other working women.

Article 12. The right to paid leave will be granted to the pregnant woman with seventy-five or more workdays, from the time when she should have been properly accredited as a worker even though she was not because of administrative negligence.

Article 13. Working women who have not worked during the period established in Article 11 of the law, will have the right to pre- and postnatal leaves, without payment, as established by the law. However, all other complementary leaves will be paid.

Unpaid Leave

Article 14. If the working woman cannot work because she must take care of her children, she will have the right to an unpaid leave of up to:

a. Nine months, if the leave starts with the expiration of the postnatal leave or any time after it. This leave will expire when the child is one year old.

b. Six months for all working mothers with children under sixteen years of age.

Article 15. Rights previously established will be granted initially for a maximum period of three months, renewable every three months if the original motive for the leave is still valid.

Article 16. If a working woman returns to work according to the terms established for the unpaid leave, she will have the right to occupy her former post.

Article 17. The administration, after hearing the opinion of the trade union local, may extend the leave when exceptional circumstances so advise, but in no case may the extension be for more than three months after the expiration of the terms established in Article 14. After this period of time, or after the extension if such is the case, the working woman will be separated and her post occupied, following the existing evaluation norms.

Article 18. In order to receive the leave regulated by paragraph b of Article 14 of these regulations, it will be indispensable for the working woman to have been hired by a workplace and have actually worked two-thirds of the workdays of the semester prior to the date of the request for leave.

In cases of new workers the trial periods will be included for the calculation of payments.

Article 19. Unpaid leave may be granted in short periods, of not less than one week, and will be accumulative until the maximum time period established is reached. If between one leave and another, the working woman works uninterruptedly for a period similar to the one established in the previous article, she will have the right to a new leave.

SECOND: All provisions which are contrary to the dispositions of the present regulations are hereby abrogated. These provisions will become effective of the date of its publication in the *Official Gazette of the Republic*.

SIGNED, In Havana, Ministry of Labor on the fifteenth day of January, 1974.

OSCAR FERNÁNDEZ PADILLA
Minister of Labor

APPENDIX B

The Family Code

Excerpt reprinted from Cuban Family Code *(New York: Center for Cuban Studies). Adopted February 14, 1975.*

Executive Branch, Council of Ministers

I, OSVALDO DORTICÓS TORRADO, president of the Republic of Cuba,

HEREBY PROCLAIM: That the Council of Ministers has approved and I have signed the following:

WHEREAS: The equality of citizens resulting from the elimination of private property over the means of production and the extinction of classes and all forms of exploitation of human beings by others is a basic principle of socialist society being constructed by our people, a principle which must be explicitly and fully reflected in the provisions of our legislation.

WHEREAS: Obsolete judicial norms from the bourgeois past which are contrary to equality and discriminatory with regard to women and children born out of wedlock still exist in our country, these norms must be replaced by others fully in keeping with the principles of equality and the realities of our socialist society, which is constantly and dynamically advancing.

WHEREAS: The socialist concept of the family is based on the fundamental consideration that it constitutes an entity in which social and personal interests are present and closely linked in view of the fact that it is the elementary cell of society and, as such, contributes to its development and plays an important role in the upbringing of the new generations. Moreover, as the center for relations of common existence between men and women and between them and their children and between all of them with their relatives, it meets deep-rooted human needs in the social field and in the field of affection for the individual.

WHEREAS: The concept expressed above and the importance which, with this in mind, our socialist society assigns to the family, make it advisable that the judicial norms on this subject be separated from other legislation and constitute the Family Code.

WHEREAS: Adoption and tutelage are institutions which normally and generally correspond to the family, it is convenient that the judicial norms which cover them be included in the Family Code, especially when the relationship between adoptive parent and adopted child is similar to that between parents and their children.

WHEREAS: The draft version of the Family Code was drawn up on the basis of the ideas and assumptions contained in the preceding whereases, by the Law Study Commission and its secretariat and presented to the deputy prime ministers, ministers, heads of central agencies, and other officials for their individual examination. Their comments and suggestions were taken into account for the improvement of the draft which had been prepared.

WHEREAS: The draft version of the Family Code was submitted for broad and far-reaching discussion by all the people through the Committees for the Defense of the Revolution, the Central Organization of Cuban Trade Unions, the Federation of Cuban Women, the National Association of Small Farmers, the Federation of University Students of Cuba, the Federation of Students of Intermediate Education, and a number of state and social agencies, and was approved in full and section by section by a majority of more than 98 percent of those who participated in the meetings and assemblies held for this purpose.

WHEREAS: In spite of the general approval, the secretariat of the Law Study Commission carefully studied each and every one of the more than 4,000 observations which were made regarding 121 of the 166 articles and, regardless of the number of those who voted for them, accepted and included in the final version all suggestions which it felt were rational and useful for the goals of the proposed legislation.

THEREFORE: By virtue of the powers vested in it the Council of Ministers has resolved to enact the following.

LAW NO. 1289
FAMILY CODE

PRELIMINARY TITLE
ON THE OBJECTIVES OF THIS CODE

Article 1. This code regulates judicially the institutions of the family—marriage, divorce, parent-child relations, obligation to provide alimony, adoption, and tutelage—with the main objections of contributing to:

• the strengthening of the family and of the ties of affection and reciprocal respect between its members;

• the strengthening of legally formalized or judicially recognized marriage, based on absolute equality of rights between men and women;

• the most effective fulfillment by parents of their obligations regarding the protection, moral upbringing, and education of their children so they can develop fully in every field as worthy citizens of a socialist society;

• the absolute fulfillment of the principle of equality of all children.

TITLE 1: MARRIAGE

Chapter 1: Marriage in General

Section 1: Marriage and its establishment

Article 2. Marriage is the voluntarily established union between a man and a woman who are legally fit to do so, in order to live together.

Marriage will have a legal effect only when it is formalized or recognized in keeping with the rules established in this code.

*Article 3.** Women and men who are over 18 years old are authorized to marry. Therefore, those who are under 18 are not authorized to marry.

In spite of the contents of the above paragraph, under special circumstances and for justified reasons, permission can be granted to those under 18 to marry, provided the girl is at least 14 and the boy at least 16.

This exceptional permission can be granted by:

1. The father and mother on a joint basis, or one of them in case the other had died or has been deprived of custody.

2. The adoptive parents or parents, in the case of adoption.

3. The tutor, if the minor is subject to tutelage.

4. The maternal or paternal grandparents without distinction, in lieu of the parents or adoptive parents, with preference given to those who live in the same dwelling as the minor.

5. One of those with the power to do so, in the case that the other person who should grant permission jointly is unable to do so.

6. The court, if, for reasons contrary to the norms and principles of socialist society, the authorized persons refuse to grant permission.

In case one of those who must grant permission jointly refuses to do so, those wishing to marry or the older brother or sister of one of them can appeal to the corresponding people's court to grant the required permission.

The court, in an oral hearing, will listen to the opinions of the interested parties and of the district attorney and, taking into account the interests of society and of those wishing to marry, will decide. The ruling of the court cannot be appealed.

Article 4. The following people will not be able to marry:

1. Those who are mentally unfit to give their consent.

2. Those who have been joined in a formalized or judicially recognized marriage.

3. Girls under 14 and boys under 16.

Article 5. The following people will not be able to marry among themselves:

1. Direct ascendants and descendants, brothers and half-brothers.

*This is the modified article as approved on August 22, 1977.

2. Those who adopted a person and the person they adopted.

3. Those who have tutelage and the person they have tutelage over.

4. Those who have been sentenced as directly responsible for the murder of the partner of either and those who have been sentenced as directly responsible for and accomplice in the murder.

Article 6. Once their marriage is ended for any reason, either of the partners has the right to formalize a new marriage anytime afterward.

However, in order to facilitate a determination of paternity, the woman whose marriage has ended and is going to formalize a new one within the next 300 days, must prove by means of a medical certificate, provided by a state medical institution, whether or not she is pregnant.

If the certificate indicates she is pregnant, the paternity of the partner in the previous marriage will be assumed. All types of legally admissible evidence can be presented to counter this assumption. If the woman has given birth before the aforementioned 300 days, no certificate will be required for the formalization of a new marriage.

Section 2: The formalization of marriage

Article 7. Those in charge of the Civil Register and notary publics are the officials who can give permission for the formalization of marriages in keeping with the provisions of this code.

Consuls and vice-consuls of the republic have the power to grant permission for marriages between Cubans abroad.

Article 8. Those who want to formalize a marriage must present and reaffirm before the official who will grant permission a statement in which, after being warned that if they do not tell the truth they are liable to the corresponding penal action, they will provide the following information:

1. First and last names.

2. Place and date of birth and the Civil Register which contains this information.

3. Citizenship, civil status, and occupation.

4. Address.

5. First and last names of their parents.

This statement is to be accompanied by a document which certifies the civil status of the applicants, whose previous marriage had been ended for any reason.

Article 9. When the permission mentioned in Article 3 is required for the formalization of a marriage it is to be granted as soon as the ratification has taken place unless it is a case of the kind covered in the last paragraph of that article, in which case the statement must be accompanied by a document which certifies that it has been granted.

Permission can also be granted as a result of an appearance before a notary public, the head of the Civil Register, consul or vice-consul, and be certified by means of the corresponding testimony or certificate which must be presented along with the initial statement.

Article 10. Marriage can be formalized by proxy when one of the partners lives in an area other than the one where the formalization is to take place.

In this case special permission indicating the name of the person with whom the marriage is to be formalized is required. This permission will be valid as long as the other partner and the proxy representative are not legally notified of the annulment of this permission before the formalization of the marriage.

Article 11. The statement mentioned in Article 8 will be included in the marriage certificate and will be reaffirmed by the partners as they formalize their marriage. It will be signed by the partners, the witnesses, and the official who grants permission for the marriage.

Article 12. The commander of a warship or the captain of a merchant ship or fishing boat will grant permission for marriages which are formalized on board, in case of imminent danger of death. The military commander of an army which is engaged in operations will also have the power to formalize marriage between members of the army, in case of imminent danger of death.

Article 13. Marriages formalized under the provisions of the above article will be conditional and subject to the factors outlined in Article 15.

Article 14. When an official who is to grant permission for a marriage suspects the existence of some legal obstacle he will listen to what the partners say and order the investigations which he feels are required and will deny or grant permission for the marriage on the basis of the results of such investigation.

Article 15. Officials with the authority to do so will authorize the marriage of those in imminent danger of death without the prior presentation of the documents which certify the aspects mentioned in the last two paragraphs of Article 8. In such cases, however, the marriage will be conditional until those documents are produced.

Article 16. The marriage will be formalized with the dignity and the solemn setting that the act requires because of its social significance. The partners—or one of them and the proxy representative—will appear before the official, together with two witnesses who are of age and not related to the partners up to the second degree of consanguinity. Then, after the official has read Articles 24-28 inclusive, he will ask each of them if they still want to formalize their marriage. If they say they do, he will provide the required certificate with all the necessary circumstances to indicate that the procedure called for in this code has been fulfilled. The marriage certificate will be signed by the partners, the witnesses, and the official who granted permission for the marriage.

Article 17. The official who grants permission for the formalization of the marriage must also take the following steps:

1. When the marriage is formalized by the head of the Civil Register, the certificate mentioned in the previous article will be entered in the book of the section which corresponds to the register in question.

2. When the marriage is formalized by a notary, he must present, within three days, a faithful copy of the certificate to the head of the Civil

Register in the place where the marriage was formalized so it can be included in the respective section of the register. He must also present the case folder established for the formalization of the marriage, with all the required documents so that it can be placed in the custody and under the care of the head of the register.

3. In cases of marriages formalized abroad in the presence of consuls and vice-consuls of the republic, the same procedure will be followed as those mentioned in clause 1 of this article. These marriages will be recorded in the Civil Register, which is administered by the General Register and Notary Department of the Ministry of Justice, and which will cover the acts and deeds that take place abroad that have to do with the civil status of Cubans or their children. Within three days of the marriage, the consul or vice-consul will send the Ministry of Justice by means of the Ministry of Foreign Affairs a certified copy of the certificate of formalization of the marriage and the case folder, to be recorded and filed in the Civil Register.

4. In the cases of marriages formalized under the provisions of Articles 12 and 13, the official who grants permission must send the certificate that has been issued for this purpose to the Ministry of Justice, within the shortest possible time.

Section 3: Nonformalized marriage

Article 18. A matrimonial union between a man and a woman who are legally fit to establish it and which is in keeping with the standards of stability and singularity, will be just as binding as legally formalized marriages when recognized by a competent tribunal.

When the matrimonial union is not singular because one of the partners was previously married, the marriage will be legally in effect for the person who acted in good faith and for the children born of that union.

Article 19. The formalization or judicial recognition of a marriage between a man and a woman who are joined together in the manner mentioned in the previous article will be retroactive to the date the union began, in keeping with the statements of the partners and the witnesses in the certificate of the formalization of the marriage or what is stated in the court decision.

Article 20. The writ of execution resulting from the process of recognition of the existence of a matrimonial union will be included in the book of the corresponding section of the Civil Register Office of the area where the partners live.

Section 4: Proof of matrimony

Article 21. Proof of a formalized or legally recognized marriage will be provided by the certificate which is recorded in the Civil Register.

Article 22. In any civil, penal, or administrative process in which the existence of a matrimonial union could not be proved according to the provisions of the previous article, according to the nature of the process, proof will be provided by constant living together, in union, along with the birth certificates of children if there are any, with the effects, in its case, of Article 18.

Article 23. Marriages formalized in foreign countries where these acts are not subject to regular or genuine registry can be proved by any legally admissible means.

Chapter II: Relations between Husband and Wife

Section 1: Rights and duties between husband and wife

Article 24. Marriage is established with equal rights and duties for both partners.

Article 25. Partners must live together, be loyal, considerate, respectful, and mutually helpful to each other.

The rights and duties that this code establishes for partners will remain in effect as long as the marriage is not legally terminated, even if the partners do not live together for any well-founded reason.

Article 26. Both partners must care for the family they have created and must cooperate with the other in the education, upbringing, and guidance of the children according to the principles of socialist morality. They must participate, to the extent of their capacity or possibilities, in the running of the home, and cooperate so that it will develop in the best possible way.

Article 27. The partners must help meet the needs of the family they have created with their marriage, each according to his or her ability and financial status. However, if one of them only contributes by working at home and caring for the children, the other partner must contribute to this support alone, without prejudice to his duty of cooperating in the above-mentioned work and care.

Article 28. Both partners have the right to practice their profession or skill and they have the duty of helping each other and cooperating in order to make this possible and to study or improve their knowledge. However, they must always see to it that home life is organized in such a way that these activities are coordinated with their fulfillment of the obligations posed by this code.

Section 2: The economic basis of matrimony

Article 29. The economic basis of matrimony will be joint property of goods as contemplated in this code.

This will prevail from the moment a marriage is formalized or from the date a union is initiated in the cases covered by Article 19 and it will cease when the marriage is terminated for any reason.

Article 30. In line with the bases mentioned in the above article, the following will be considered joint property:

1. The salaries or wages, retirement pensions, benefits, and other pensions or other income obtained by one or both partners during the marriage as a result of work done or from the social security fund.

2. The goods and the rights acquired by virtue of a purchase made during the marriage with common funds, regardless of whether the

purchased item is for joint use or for one of the partners.

3. The benefits, rents, or interests received or acquired during the marriage from goods or items which are considered joint property or those which are the individual property of either partner.

Article 31. The goods in the possession of the partners will be presumed to be common property as long as it is not proven that they are the sole property of one or the other.

Article 32. The following items are the property of the partners individually:

1. Those purchased by either one prior to the marriage.

2. Those they purchased during the marriage with money derived from inheritance, in replacement or substitution of another item which is their property, and for commercial purposes. In cases of donations and onerous payment made with funds which are common property, a deduction will be made.

3. Those which were purchased with the money of one of the partners.

4. The money collected by one or the other partner in periods during the marriage that is the result of an amount or credit in his or her favor previous to the marriage and payable in a specific number of installments.

5. Those which are for the exclusive use of each of the partners.

Section 3: Responsibilities and obligations involved in joint property of goods

Article 33. The joint property of goods will involve the following responsibilities:

1. Support of the family and meeting of the expenses resulting from the education and upbringing of children of both or one of the partners.

2. All debts and obligations arising during the marriage that were taken on and assumed by either partner, except in the cases when the consent of both was required to assume them.

3. The rent or interests derived during the marriage from the obligations to which the goods that were the property of the individual partners and those which are joint property are subject.

4. Minor repair work or upkeep of individual property during the marriage.

Article 34. The payment of the debts assumed by either partner before marriage will not have to be covered by joint property.

Section 4: Administration of joint property

Article 35. The partners are the ones who must administer their joint property and either of them may be in charge of administration and the purchase of goods which, due to their nature, are destined for ordinary use or consumption by the family.

Article 36. Neither partner may have control over goods which are joint property without the consent of the other, except when it is to satisfy a demand posed by the community.

Article 37. In all cases not covered in this code, the joint property of goods will be governed by the general provisions that cover joint property.

Section 5: The termination and liquidation of joint property of goods

Article 38. The joint property of goods will be ended by the termination of the marriage. Joint property will be divided up in half between the partners or, in case of death, between the survivor and the heirs of the deceased.

When the marriage is terminated by its being declared null and void, the partner whose bad faith brought this about will not share in the distribution of joint property.

Either partner may forfeit his rights, in full or in part, to the joint property after the marriage has been terminated. This must always be done in writing.

Article 39. When no agreement can be reached among the interested parties for the termination of joint property in the manner indicated in the previous article and it becomes necessary to resort to a court settlement, an inventory and appraisal of the goods will be made, based on their value when the marriage was terminated.

Once the appraisal is carried out, all debts pending, obligations, and responsibilities will be deducted and what is left will be distributed in the proportion indicated in the previous article.

Article 40. One year after termination of the marriage resulting from divorce or annulment, if the legal or extralegal measures for the termination of joint property have not been initiated without prejudice to what is contained in the second paragraph of Article 38, the partners will remain the only owners of the personal property, real estate, or joint property in their possession since the termination.

Article 41. In spite of the provisions of previous articles, the court, when ordering the liquidation of joint property, may decide that certain domestic items of common property which it feels are needed or convenient for the education and upbringing of minor children be given with preference to the partner who has custody over the children. If this gives him more than half the goods, he will be given the right to use the excess even though the other partner retains ownership over it as long as he or she acquires similar items.

Article 42. In case the marriage is terminated because of death, the surviving partner and the minor children have the right to continue using the common property until legal action is taken to terminate the joint property of goods. The court that has jurisdiction over the matter will grant permission, to the extent that it is necessary, for the surviving partner to receive the payments which corresponded to the deceased or to the joint property, so that using these funds or the money which is part of the goods that have been left, the ordinary expenses of the surviving partner and those of the minor children can be met and the necessary withdrawals from the bank accounts of the deceased or of both can be made in order to fulfill that obligation.

Chapter III: Termination of Marriage

Section 1: General provisions

Article 43. The bonds of matrimony are terminated:
1. By the death of the husband or wife.
2. By a court order on the presumed death of husband or wife.
3. By an unappealable judgment of annulment.
4. By an unappealed decree of divorce.

Section 2: On the presumed death of husband or wife

*Article 44.** The court order on the presumed death of one of the partners terminates the marriage as of the moment when it goes into effect. If the remaining spouse does not marry again and the one presumed dead reappears, the marriage will be declared valid if so requested by both at the Civil Register. Otherwise, they will be considered divorced. In the case of the remaining spouse having married again, the marriage will be considered legal, and the civil status of the one who reappeared will be equivalent to that of a divorced person.

Section 3: Annulment of marriage

Article 45. Marriaged formalized under the following are declared null:
1. Violation of any of the prohibitions contained in Articles 4 and 5.
2. Marriage to the wrong person or under coercion or intimidation to bring about consent.
3. Infringement of the requisites established by this code to declare a marriage legal.

Article 46. Action to request annulment of marriage must be taken by:
1. Either of the partners, or the district attorney in the case of clauses 1 and 2 of the preceding article.
2. By the partner who was victim of the error, coercion, or intimidation in the case of clause 2 of the preceding article.

Article 47. Action for annulment shall be taken within six months of the formalization of marriage in the cases pointed out in Article 3 and clauses 2 and 3, Article 45.

If action is not taken within the six-month period the marriage will be validated as a matter of law.

In the case of clause 3, Article 4, the marriage will be validated as a matter of law if both minors reach the established age without action for annulment having been taken or the female is pregnant.

A marriage formalized with any of the vices contained in clauses 1 and 2, Article 4, and in Article 5, cannot be validated and action for annulment may be taken at any time.

Article 48. A marriage declared null will yield, in any case, the rights stated in this code for the children resulting from said marriage and for the partner who has acted in good faith.

*This is the modified article as approved on August 22, 1977.

If both partners have acted in bad faith, the marriage will yield no rights in favor of either of them.

The partner who at the time when the marriage was formalized knew of the existence of any cause for annulment is considered to have acted in bad faith.

Good faith is presumed, unless the contrary is proved.

Section 4: Divorce

Article 49. Divorce will result in the dissolution of the matrimonial ties and all the other effects mentioned in this section.

Article 50. Divorce can only be obtained by means of a judicial decree.

Article 51. Divorce will take effect by common agreement or when the court determines that there are factors which have led the marriage to lose its meaning for the partners and for the children and, thus, for society as a whole.

Article 52. For the purposes of this law it is understood that marriage loses its meaning for the partners and for the children and, thus, for society as a whole when there are causes which create an objective situation in which the marriage is no longer, or cannot be in the future, the union of a man and a woman in a manner adequate to exercise the rights, fulfill the obligations, and obtain the objectives mentioned in Articles 24-28 inclusively.

Article 53. Either one of the partners can take action to obtain a divorce.

Article 54. The divorce action can be taken at any time as long as the situation which motivated it exists.

Article 55. The divorce will have the following effects between the partners:

1. Termination of their marriage, as of the day the court decree becomes definitive.

2. Separation of property of the partners, following liquidation of the joint property of goods, which is to be carried out in keeping with the rules established in Section Five, Chapter II, Title I of this code.

3. Termination of the right of succession among the partners.

Article 56. If the partners have lived together for more than a year or if children have been born during their marriage, the court, when handing down the decree of divorce, will grant an alimony for one of them in the following cases:

1. The partner who does not have a paying job and lacks other means of support. This will be temporary and it will be paid by the other partner for six months if there are no minor children in his or her care and guardianship, or for a year if there are, so the beneficiary can obtain a paying job.

2. The partner who because of age, disability, illness, or other insurmountable obstacles is unable to work and lacks other means of support. In this case the alimony will continue as long as the obstacle exists.

Article 57. In the decree of divorce the court will grant custody establishing as a rule that both parents shall retain it over their minors.

However, the court may grant it to the parent whom it feels should have it, when this is required by the interests of the minors, outlining the reasons why one or the other is deprived of it.

Likewise, the court may determine, outlining its basis for doing so, the negation of custody to both parents when this is necessary for the interests of the children, in which case the children will be placed under tutelage.

Article 58. In the decree of divorce the court must determine which of the parents will have guardianship and care over the children born during the marriage and will take the necessary measures so the children can maintain adequate communication with the parent that is not entrusted with their guardianship and care.

For the purposes of the provisions in the previous paragraph, the court will be guided by the rules established in Articles 88, 89, and 90.

Article 59. Support of minors is a duty of both parents even if they do not have custody over them or even if the children are not under their guardianship and care or even if they are enrolled in an educational institution. In accordance with this norm, the court, in its decree of divorce, will set the amount of alimony to be paid by the parent who does not have the minors under his or her guardianship and care.

Article 60. The amount of alimony for minors will be determined by their normal expenses and the income of the parents, in order to determine the responsibility of the latter in a proportionate manner.

Article 61. The measures contained in decrees of divorce regarding alimony, custody, guardianship and care, and communications can be modified whenever it is deemed necessary because the circumstances which led to their being adopted have changed.

Article 62. For the temporary measures adopted during the course of the divorce action with regard to guardianship and care, communication with the children, and alimony for them, and, if necessary, for one of the partners, the rules established in this section are to be observed.

These measures can be changed during the process if a reason for doing so materializes.

Article 63. Proof of a divorce will be provided by a copy of the court order issued by a competent tribunal or its recording in the Civil Register.

Article 64. A divorce obtained abroad which terminates marriage, held according to the laws of that country or according to Cuban laws between Cubans or between a Cuban and a foreigner, or between foreigners, will be valid in Cuba as long as the Cuban consulate in the country where it was granted certifies that it was substantiated and granted according to the laws of that country.

List of Initials

ANAP—Asociación Nacional de Agricultores Pequeños, National Association of Small Farmers

CDR—Comités de Defensa de la Revolución, Committees for the Defense of the Revolution

CTC—Central de Trabajadores de Cuba, Central Organization of Cuban Trade Unions

FAR—Fuerzas Armadas Revolucionarias, Revolutionary Armed Forces

FMC—Federación de Mujeres Cubanas, Federation of Cuban Women

FOC—Facultad Obrera-Campesina, Worker-Peasant Faculty

INIT—Instituto Nacional de la Industria Turística, National Institute of Tourism

MINCIN—Ministerio de Comercio Interior, Ministry of Domestic Commerce

MINED—Ministerio de Educación, Ministry of Education

MININT—Ministerio del Interior, Ministry of the Interior

MINSAP—Ministerio de Salud Pública, Ministry of Public Health

PCC—Partido Comunista de Cuba, Communist Party of Cuba

UJC—Unión de Jóvenes Comunistas, Young Communist League

Index

- July 26 movement
- Mariana Grajales Platoon